THE MARKETPROS VISION

To transform the Real Estate Industry by building a bridge of trust between Real Estate professionals and consumers through equipping professionals with the habits, ethics, attitudes, and knowledge of a MarketPro so that they become easily referable, highly trusted, and widely known in their community among both buyers and sellers

"The Danger Report" was a study paid for by the National Association of REALTORS© which determined that the number #1 biggest issue was that "Masses of Marginal Agents Destroy Reputation". The real estate industry is saddled with a large number of part-time, untrained, unethical, and/or incompetent agents. This knowledge gap threatens the credibility of the industry, a major factor in me not only writing this book, but also in trying to change the way people look at Real Estate Professionals one agent at a time. Thus, forming a new movement in Real Estate would encourage those people to become a Market Pro where the consumers can be sure they are dealing with the best in their area.

It really does not matter where you live to be able to earn over $100,000 or more per year as a Market Pro in the Real Estate Industry, even if you do just some of the things in this book. My biggest message that has helped many is aligning your Habits, Ethics, Attitude and Resilience to gain Trust. My acronym is HEART, and you will see an amazing difference as to how many more people will be attracted to you and will seek you out because of it. The tips and stories in this book just touch on a little bit of what a Market Pro is and what they can do to give the Real Estate Industry back the reputation it once had.

Remember that according to another recent report from the NAR, only 16% of Real Estate Professionals earned more than $100,000, and with 8% earning more than $150,000. We need to be honest that the fact is 55% of these very wealthy 8% are Market Pro Real Estate Professionals who have been in the industry for more than 16 years, including myself. There are obviously things we have learned and you can too, that have contributed to our success as a Market Pro. Hope this book helps.

Sincerely, Kerry Jayne Jackson

Marketpros.com

FORWARD: *Dedicated to my once client, now special friend Robert Drake who has consistently, believed in me, supported me, told me how good I really was and encouraged me to stay in Real Estate and actually came up with the idea with me after my event in Tampa in 2014. He helped me with my message I am sharing with you in this book.*

Harvard University and their studies on psychology, behavior, and persuasion so that I learned how to better understand human beings and serve them through my business.

Anthony Kovic, my videographer for my 1st Speaking event, personally made me stay with this and became a mentor, a friend, my editor and my inspiration during some challenging times when I thought for a minute this was too big of a dream.

My Mastermind Buddies from Board of Advisors thank you for keeping me on task and helping me with the things I didn't know.

My son Brady for being my assistant and helping keep the business going while I write this and planned the whole Market Pros idea to move forward over the past 2 years.

My Mom who always told me I could do whatever I set my mind to do. I know you are watching from Heaven.

Let's Start

What is The Difference between a Real Estate Agent, A Real Estate Professional and a Market Pro?

These titles used by the general public are a "real estate agent" and a "Real Estate Professional". They are often used interchangeably. A "Market Pro" is both of the above on Steroids as they will not only go above and beyond, they have documented reviews. They have already accomplished that, with not just 5 years' continuous experience but also by residing or working in the area where they help people for the past 5 years which gives them the knowledge of area and area zonings and politics which is so important in this industry. They know when a new business is coming to town and when construction is starting on a road or a wastewater treatment plant. They know where you are allowed to have rentals and where you are not before you buy. A Market Pro is important to the Buyers and Sellers who don't have the time to work with Real Estate Professionals or Real Estate agents that are just learning themselves or only work part time, who could potentially lead them down the wrong path or waste a lot of their time because they just don't know the area.

Why do people use the terms interchangeably if they mean different things?

Because using the term "real estate agent" can be a mouthful and wordy as well, and those who may not be familiar with the differences between the two designations often use the term "Real Estate Professional" as a slang to refer to anyone who is in the business of helping people buy and sell real estate. A "Market Pro" is a Real Estate Agent who has a minimum of 5 years fulltime experience and has lived in the area they List and Sell for a minimum of 5 years as well. They have high D and I level in their DISC test.

But they are different — right? All three, Real Estate Agents, REALTORS and Market Pros are licensed through their State to sell real estate, each title refers to a specific type of real estate professional, and there are certain notable differences between the three.

Marketpros.com

A Real Estate Agent is someone who is holding a license to help people buy and sell commercial or residential property. The agent may do so as a real estate sales person, an associate broker or a broker. There is a difference if you belong to NAR.

A REALTOR is a trademarked name for a licensed agent who is part of a large group that is under the National Association of Realtors (NAR). To date, there are over a million.

They pay dues to an Association similar to a Union. They pay dues and have a single large voice in lobbying and in government matters and causes to do with charity or publicity. They are held to stricter ethics rules and governances than real estate agents, but not enforced very well. They have Multiple Listing Services for other Real Estate Professionals to search for properties.

Where does the term "REALTOR" come from?

NAR was founded more than a century ago, but it has only used the term "REALTOR" for about 40 years. The association was originally founded in 1908 as the "National Association of Real Estate Exchanges" and changed its name in 1916 to "The National Association of Real Estate Boards".

That was the year a guy named, Charles N. Chadbourn, a real estate agent in Minneapolis and vice president of the National Association of Real Estate Boards, initiated the use of the term "REALTOR" to give members of the association a way to tell themselves apart from non-members. Similar to what I am trying to do with initiating the term MarketPros with Real Estate Professionals who meet the criteria to be a MarketPro.

To protect the title from misuse, the association obtained a copyright and trademark on it in 1950.

The NAR association came up with its current name in 1974. Headquartered in Chicago, NAR has more than 1 million members across the country – and membership is not restricted to only real estate agents and brokers. Members may also be property managers, appraisers, real estate counselors and other professionals involved in the real estate industry. It can be a very stressful but lucrative business.

MARKET PROS was an idea that was conveyed in an event in Tampa in 2014 but the name Marketpros was conceived in 2015 and is in the midst of attempting to get a trademark and copyright for distinguishing experienced, successful, knowledgeable and professional Real Estate Professionals who could be either RE Agent or Real Estate Professional with any company. They will have to prove they have been a fulltime Real Estate Professional or Agent consistently for the past 5 years and have lived in the market they serviced for the past 5 years or 6 out of the past 10 years. They will average 12 sales a year or more individually or a Million in sales. Not their team unless all members of the team meet that criteria.

There are some other criteria, that will refer to verified reviews from other people in their circle. There will be semi-annual events to encourage other agents to become Market Pros. This is just the beginning. I am a big thinker and believe the need for this in today's Real Estate world is so necessary to preserve this occupation. This has been echoed over the years by other Real Estate Professionals who are Market Pros. Here is what another agent sent me when I explained my mission of creating a new designation for Real Estate Professionals and Agents.

"As a licensed Real Estate Professional for 20 years, I have seen that there are only a handful of Agents and Brokers who stand out from the rest. There are so many lacking local knowledge and integrity to say the least. Kerry Jackson's concept for Market Pros is a great one and it is very important for not only the consumers out there but for the reputation of the entire Real Estate Industry as a whole. I have successfully worked many deals with Kerry and I am always inspired by her attitude no matter what the situation is to resolve issues and get them done. She remains genuine and friendly throughout the entire deal. The market pro concept is a revolutionary one that I personally think would help all Real Estate Professionals better themselves." - Mario Goebel

Marketpros.com

As you might not know, my name is Kerry Jackson. This was the year I sold 68 million over 88 transactions, administrative assistant and I alone. I am here at a party where I was recognized at an awards ceremony.

The reason I have written this book is a twofold. Number one, obviously, was that I feel I can help everyone who has taken the huge and brave step by opening this book and telling yourself you are committed to becoming a true Market Pro. I am here from a purpose of trying to serve and make a change in the way Real Estate Professionals are portrayed in today's marketplace. Of course, the other reason is the protection of the consumers who want to know there is a place to look up a Market Pro and be assured they are working with someone who knows their stuff.

Everybody has challenges and I'm hoping I can overcome them with what I do know by coming up with live panels and solutions for 100's of scenarios that have been considered deal busters or challenges. I have made my share of mistakes over the years and have realized that. As a matter of fact, citing the Chinese proverb "A journey of a thousand miles begins with a single step", I have had to walk 2,000 miles before I took the right step to being successful in this business. I would love to see that I prevented some of you from taking a misstep and preventing you from putting on the same mileage I did on my original journey. You do not have to. I want to inspire average agents, who are struggling to make a living and are turning to part time and fulltime jobs but have the passion, open mindfulness and knowledge of being in this business.

It has been really a challenge for me to take this stuff from my heart and my head (both your brains) and put it into some formula that can help everybody who is a struggling average Real Estate Professional or Agent, one who up to this point really didn't know what it takes to have constant leads coming in from referrals, doesn't make more than 100k a year and one who does not know what to say when what seems like an insurmountable challenge comes up in your transaction you are attempting to close. Someone who is not yet a Market Pro, but is reading or listening to this because they know they have it in them to become one and desire to do so. They just need a little polishing.

Points brought up by the National Association of Real Estate Professionals in their very own reports substantiate the need for this book, the need to ensure Real Estate Professionals are actually operating from the same guidelines both inside and out on a regular basis. Have some sort of monitoring system or better testing, something other than memorizing some information on Real Estate so they can pass a test and then be responsible in people buying the most important and most expensive item in their entire life. We are talking an average of at least $100,000.00. Did you know that in the state of Florida, one in every 175 people hold a valid Florida Real Estate License? Brokers are supposed to be doing this training but they just are all not doing it. Sure they teach you how to write a contract but not how to look after yourself or the consumer with what's inside of you. Some are just about the numbers and the money before any of this is ever thought about.

Would you trust a bookkeeper with a $100,000 IRS problem or would you go to a CPA who has experience in that area?

Marketpros.com

Wouldn't you want an expert in this field who knew what they were doing?

Can you imagine going to the dentist saying "well I only do this part time because I don't make enough money to do it fulltime". So, if I am not as informed as other dentists, I apologize ahead of time. I would run and so should the average Buyer and Seller in today's market when a licensed agent has no experience. Currently, they can go out and do their own thing and who would know. They can be a week out of school and promote themselves online as being in the top 3% and no one polices what they say.

(Look up the "Danger Report NAR" in a search engine and read it. Then you will understand)

But I want to tell you the other reason why I'm writing this. I want to tell you a bit about how I got into real estate and what I am sharing with you, I've been through. When I started in the real estate business at 40 years old, I was in professional sales. I was selling in the telecommunications business in 1997, had been in sales prior and also owned my own businesses.

Somebody said, "You would do great at real estate. You need to get into real estate. No, you really do. You'll make a lot of money."

So to me, when someone said a lot of money back then I said, "I'm making six figures in sales." They said, "No, lots of money in real estate. You can make a fortune." I went, "Okay. Well, maybe that's what I need to do." I did both for a while Real Estate and my sales job. A no-no in this business.

I should have listened to Andrew Carnegie, the second richest man ever, who revolutionized the steel business in the late 1800's. He said, "As I grow older, I pay less attention to what men say. ... No man will make a great leader who wants to do it all himself or get all the credit for doing it. ... The way to become rich is to put all your eggs in one basket and then watch that basket."

For those of you that think you can do both, you can't and don't. You will end up dropping all the baskets and the eggs inside will be ruined and you won't make any money on them. There are only so many hours in a day and it is not about how many things you can do, but how many things you can do well. Think of it this way. If your doctor also worked as a bartender at the local night club and only worked 1 or 2 days a week or whenever he was scheduled off his other job, how much trust would you have that he knew what he was doing. If you go part time, majority of people will not take you serious enough to trust you in that business and secondly, this is not meant to be a part time career. Real estate is a lifestyle. It means you are available and open to meeting people anytime day or night to work around their schedule. If you are not available, there are plenty of others to call.

Sometimes you can call the shots if it's a repeat client or if you have already formed a relationship online or over the phone with them or if they already are aware you are a MarketPro. Like going to a specialist when your doctor refers you, it always takes a lot longer to get an appointment. I am providing some great scripts that you can make your own throughout the book that covers a lot of situations you might encounter.

I went out and got my real estate license in 2000. I put my license with a Real Estate Broker. My first year, I made $30,000. I would remember going into the office and sitting there at floor time, because this is what they told you to do. That was how it was before the Internet was part of the Industry. We had binders with listings back then. They gave me the books. They gave me all the information. They said, "Here, read this and sit here. Eventually, you will get some business." And, I made $30,000. I'm saying to myself, "Self, this is not for me. This real estate business is not for me." I would have starved had I not found a mentor who had been in the business a while. I just worked in the same office as him and paid attention to what he said and did and what he didn't do. I didn't split commissions with him, I just was a fly on the wall so to speak but I sat in a chair at a desk next to his. Like being an apprentice which I think is needed in this industry.

Marketpros.com

He was like a coach and Barry Zweig is a friend to this day although I only stayed one year there. I believe everybody needs one of those especially if you are new in this business, or if you have been in the business but you want to start all over again. I think by you reading this book, I can help you realize you can make more than the average Real Estate Professional who at the time of writing this book is $47,700.00 a year.

In saying that., in the beginning of my real estate life, I was able to luckily find out from him how he did it. He said, "Kerry, why don't you go back and look at why you were so successful in all your previous sales jobs? How did you make six figures in sales when most of the sales people in your industry only make $60,000 to $70,000 a year?"

I had to think. I'm like, "Well, I don't know. I really didn't know". I had no idea, because all I was thinking about was money at that time. Because I was so strapped at $30,000 a year when I was used to making a $160,000 a year, I couldn't even think straight. My mindset was one of scarcity another important lesson I learned from another mentor of mine, Les Brown who you will see in this book. You see, when I was trying to do both, my sales fell. It is hard to do two careers at one time and do them both really well. I had to learn to not only focus but go with the flow and take action. You will hear me mention that many times throughout this book, as taking action is one of the common denominators of the top 5% of Real Estate agents who are Market Pros, worldwide. I went to seminars, I spoke to other successful agents, I read books on things that I didn't know about. I learned all the zoning laws for the area and got to know the Planners and Inspectors. No Search Engines back then, the only engine I had back then was the one in my car.

I went to some of my customers from the previous company. I said, "Can I just ask you a big favor? Can you tell me what it was why you did business with me when I was in telecommunications?" They said, "We trusted you, explicitly." "Why did you trust me, though?"

They said, "Because you had a big heart. We knew that you were doing things ethically. We knew that where you were coming from it wasn't always about the money for you. You had a great attitude all the time. You came in and you were always positive. You never once mentioned anything negative. Even though we had problems and there were things that happened, you always jumped back up and run to help us all the time even if there is no money in it for you." I can still call on any of those people today over 25 years later. (hence why my acronym is HEART)

I got that feedback from more than one customer. I just took that information. I just carried on my real estate career using that information. I leveraged my past relationships which I had not thought of doing. The following year, I made a $140,000 a year in real estate just from taking that information that I learned, from going from 30k to 140k. That was back in 2001 or 2002.

In saying that, obviously my main focus is what I'm trying to communicate to you. It is creating relationships. Learning how to build and maintain relationships that will stay with you for the rest of your career and the rest of your life. It's not just in business. It's in your personal life as well, because your personal life reflects on your business life and vice versa. Your inner and outer world must be aligned with your HEART. Heart stands for Habits, Ethics, Attitude, Resilience, Trust.

As you know in real estate, every person you meet is a customer. I dare, if somebody could tell me right now, somebody you would possibly run into that is not possibly or could be a customer, know a customer, refer you a customer, have somebody that's going to buy a house, that's going to sell a house, that needs advice on a home or mortgage for a friend or relative.

There's not one human being out there in this universe, anywhere, that is not going to at some time, know somebody you could potentially be doing business with.

Perfect example, my last colonoscopy, while I was lying there about to be put under, I overheard the nurse saying, "I heard you're a Real Estate Professional." I was like, "Yes." I'm thinking to myself, "Where's my card?"

Marketpros.com

Instead, I said, "You've got my information. I'm lying here. I've got no clothes on. I know you have my information." She said, "No, privacy act. The "HIPAA Law." We can't do that."

When I finished, the first thing, when I awoke from my anesthesia, was to look for my purse and get my cards and find her. She actually contacted me. I was there to help her. She just didn't know how to do it. I've solved her problem. You would be surprised how many people really don't know the steps to buying a home. Don't you feel good every time you do something nice for someone else and being able to do it well is even better.

"A Beautiful thing happens when we start paying attention to each other. It is by participating more in your relationship that you breathe life into it." - Steve Maraboli. Photo is my Dad at 80yrs old and my son Taylor 17 yrs. old at the time helping him put his water pump back together.

13

"YOUR LIFESTYLE, YOUR MINDSET"

Here are the most important things (I think anyway) of what you should know about in the Real Estate business if you want to achieve an income over $100,000 per year and to find out how to balance out between Real Estate and your personal life.

You must put time in. But don't call it work, it somehow makes a difference. There is no secret here. You have to have the passion, love what you do and you will never work another day in your life. In order to meet your goals, you also need to have HEART, Good Habits, Ethics, Attitude, Resilience and Trust. It can be fun work. If you think it's hard, it will be. Success does not lead to Happiness; Happiness leads to Success.

In life, when we ask for trouble, it usually comes to us, not always in the form of what we think trouble is. We get what we ask for, most of the time. If we walk around with a chip on our shoulder, constantly have a bad attitude, and are always angry about something, we most likely will receive the same in return. When you smile at someone, they will 99% of time smile back at you and when you give someone a hateful look you will most likely get a hateful look back. However, when we project kindness, good attitude, and a service of giving to others, we get two-fold in return of kindness, good attitude, service from others. We get what we ask for, we get what we wish for, and we get what we live for. If you know these things, it helps so much with the stress levels when unforeseen things happen, like your teenager who all of a sudden has a problem that you can't fix it yourself or someone you trusted does something that makes you wonder if they are truly your friend. A home inspector says the AC needs servicing right after it has been serviced. You have to also laugh at some of these things instead of getting stressed. Find the lesson, which in the last case is never use that Home Inspector again.

When you know your HEART is aligned, it makes it easier to deal with things that would cause drama for you and others and expend energy that could otherwise be used for helping yourself so you can be strong enough to help others.

Marketpros.com

The IDEA for our life with others is simple. Use our life to teach others with our daily routine. Actions speak louder than words. It is more important to be the message instead of giving it. We should always be on our best behavior, in the private times and in the public times. What you do privately will become public. This is what I consider "Living from the inside out". This way of behaving and lifestyle has to become a habit for a Market Pro and although we sometimes get out of alignment, when we get distracted with things that happen., We must remember that they are only a distraction, which will last as long as you allow it to.

We see this so much in our world today. We all have known Real Estate Professionals who say one thing, but do something entirely different when they think no one is watching. You can't hide your true self, so make sure your true self is who you want to become. Our life becomes a Demonstration. We should model the truth in the way we speak because others are observing our actions and words. We live in a show-and-tell world. So put your best foot forward always, with family, work and community. If you slip up go back as soon as possible and say something, apologize.

Allow others to experience the joy and love you have within you. Remembering you cannot change people, places or things but you can share with them how to participate and apply these traits to their life. As we practice being kind, generous, faithful, loving and hopeful, invite them along for the journey, sharing the experience. Help them understand where they are growing and help provide them direction and focus. It is our duty to each other to instruct, demonstrate, experience and assess life to its fullest and to help each other and in turn reach our potential. A client asked me recently if I could speak to her 27-year-old son as he was looking for a job and was not having any luck. I met him for 2 hours and inspired him to look at different opportunities he had never thought about it. I just let him know that thinking big and feeding your mind with good books, that will help you get to where you want to go. I suggested he get out of the box and rebuild a new one for himself that was much bigger. He gave me a hug and thanked me. It made me feel so good.

I encourage us to go into life from today forward with the idea that we will use our gifts and talents to tackle the issues that seem to stop others, a true sign of a Market Pro. Sometimes an issue that is large to one person may be simple or small to another. Step up. Take charge, put your head down and run through the obstacle or work past the distraction that could be holding others or even you back from reaching your full potential. I am hoping that you will make a difference and add value to others starting today. I hope you have the same happen to you.

I love what the founder of Spartan Race Joe De Sena said in "**How do you overcome obstacles?**

"Whether you're running 100 miles or running a business – and I would argue that running a business is a lot harder than running 100 miles – it's all about being in the right frame of mind. Often, it's not a matter of IF things are going to get ugly; it's a matter of WHEN. The way I get through those pain points is by treating every situation as a learning opportunity and reminding myself that it could always be worse. If you keep things in perspective and leave your ego out of it, then it just becomes a matter of putting one foot in front of the other."

Creating and Accepting your Lifestyle

"If you see some special life outside of daily activities, that is like brushing aside waves to look for water" - Wu Chun

Real Estate is a Lifestyle and we will make mistakes. I've made many of them over the years, but if you call it a mistake, it means you haven't learned from it. I can remember in my 1st year trying to get a hold of the sellers agent as my Buyer was "gung ho" and wanted to buy this house and because the Sellers who were present while I was showing suggested we do it now. Sellers said don't worry about my agent. It was a full price offer so I saw no harm at the time, plus I knew the other Broker. Big mistake. I could have been in big trouble if the other Broker had not known me well enough to know it was a mistake and I would never intentionally hurt anyone. He forgave me and never reported it. Thank you Scott.

Marketpros.com

Mistakes are what make people successful. I've heard that the more mistakes you make the more successful you become. Failure provides opportunity for happiness and success. However in Real Estate it can lead to lawsuits. That's the stressful part sometimes. I have a story for that.

When Getting Frustrated in this Industry

When you need something to pick you up every now and then, practice gratitude. Sincere personal gratitude for what you have, instead of what you don't have. I always think of Nick whom I met a few times through Les Brown. Nick Vujicic is an Inspiration to a lot of People with no legs or arms he is the poster child for being a Victor not a Victim. His book is called, "No Arms, No Legs, No Worry" Watch his videos on you tube and feel inspired and grateful.

Also, go to Ted.com for inspiration each day. My favorite or get a Tony Robins app or a Market Pros app that delivers a small bit of advice, motivation or insight daily. Listen to great books that feed your mind with good stuff on Audible.com. Hang out befriend other Market Pros in this business and let them help you with the things you need help with. Another quote from Andrew Carnegie makes perfect sense especially in this business.

"As I grow older, I pay less attention to what men say. I just watch what they do."

"No man will make a great leader who wants to do it all himself, or to get all the credit for doing it. "
"People who are unable to motivate themselves must be content with mediocrity, no matter how impressive their other talents."

If you have forgotten how good it feels to do something nice for someone else, things to put you in a good mood, I can list a couple of things that work great, like smiling at someone who doesn't look happy and saying how much you like their eyes or dress or tie. Or opening a door for someone at a store. It's a law of the Universe that when you help someone else, by default you are really helping yourself.

As I've said, if you're aligned and living from the inside out all the time, which is my main message, which I'll go through a lot of the marketing stuff, but this is the key thing for me which I say is probably my biggest thing that has helped me make the money that I make is having my habits, ethics, attitude, resilience to gain trust. You have to have the first four aligned in order to gain the trust. My acronym is HEART.

If you're not living from the inside out on a regular basis, you're probably not going to be quite as successful as you could be in this Real Estate World today without it. That is one of the things that I feel is most important. "Your Clients may NOT remember what you said to them or what you did for them, but they WILL remember how you made them feel".

But I'll go on. There's three things that you have. Did you all like it? Does it make sense? It's like that with everything. As I said, as you're going through, even in the grocery store, a lot of times we might not be in a great mood if we're in a rush or something. But if you think, if you're truly living from the inside

Marketpros.com

out, you're not going to be upset at the girl behind the counter for cutting your meat too thick. You're going to be okay with it. Ok, here's an example, when we were making phone calls to some of the agents in Tampa area to let them know about the event I did, some of them would start off the conversation going, "Hi, this is Mary from... Can I help you?" Very pleasant, very nice. As soon as they said, "Well, we were just checking to see if you were going to be able to..." "Where are you from? What are you doing?" Like, "Why are you calling me?"

Now, that's not somebody who's living from... sometimes we tend to do that if we're in the middle of doing something else. It would have been so much easier to just say, "Listen, I'm terribly busy. I don't have a chance to listen to you. Could you call me back or can you send me an email?" That would have been the appropriate thing that I would have said.

I get calls all the time. "Do you want to buy oil and gas?" "Do you want to invest in a movie?" Because when you start making money, trust me, people will find out you're making money. Then, they'll start calling you on a regular basis. You'll have to learn how to say, be polite and say, "I'm sorry. I can't do that."

But what you do have to offer your customers is you actually have three things. You don't have any vehicles to sell. You don't have any shoes to sell them. You don't have any inventory or product yourself so to speak.

When you meet somebody, you really don't have anything tangible to sell them at that time but you do have your time, you have your knowledge, and you have your heart. You have to have those three things. In what order? It is totally up to you. There is also nothing more rewarding than getting a text or email thanking you or saying how awesome you are. It happens a lot if you are truly successful at Living from the Inside Out.

> "Attract what you expect, reflect what you desire, become what you respect, mirror what you admire."

    If you want to be fulltime in this business, one thing is for sure. You are going to be a marketer as well, because in order to get in front of some of these people, sometimes you have to find a way to attract them in the beginning if you don't have existing relationships from past careers or jobs.

    I want to say something about this too. Back before the internet or when the internet first evolved, at that time people could send out emails or advertising through the internet, and people would automatically open any and every email and you would be able to get them to communicate back with you or they would buy pretty well what you were selling if it was of value.

    But in today's world, there's 3,000+ of those people emailing you because now that everybody's doing it, it's not a novelty anymore. Drip campaigns and CRM's are the way to go. Sending out regular marketing stuff over email does not work as well. You actually have to have something that's going to attract them. You know what I'm saying? There are other ways that you have to give them Value. Same goes for Facebook, you need to offer something of Value, not talk about yourself.

Marketpros.com

We're going to show you how to add value... Have you ever gone to buy a car but just wanted to look first and then do your research, similar to what people do when they are looking to buy Real Estate? Then you start getting bombarded with emails asking you if you are ready to buy or just touching base is lame, they really want to sell you. I can't stand that. If they had sent me a report showing me something of VALUE, like the best time of year to buy and why, how to use your vehicle as a tax write off etc., I would have saved his emails and been more likely to go back to him when I was ready. In Real Estate, it is the same way. Why can't you send to a list renters a recent news articles about the area Real Estate or how much tax can you save by owning, the difference between renting and owning, or the last homes sold in the area. Just something that would be something they would read and say, "Thanks I didn't know that". Let the knowledge inside you help educate your clients. They too will keep your emails as a reference maybe so when they have gained enough knowledge from YOU. It will be in their computers still and they will go back to YOU as the Market Pro they trust. I used to send out motivational stories or really good pictures of the area or keep the out of town buyers up to date on results from hurricanes or storms nearby.

Sales people will sell clients what they already have. Marketers make sure that they have what clients want in order to buy. What do you have again? What are the three things you have?

Time, Knowledge, Heart.

Those are the three things you have. That's who the clients are going to want to buy from. They're going to want to spend time, spend their money on people they know. Listen to them, they have the time. They have the knowledge, and they have a good heart, that they can trust. Real Estate is the biggest purchase most people make in their whole life.

When you're spending hundreds of thousands of dollars, you wouldn't get on an airplane if the pilot had just read a book. While I got my license, I read the book, I passed the test, trust me with your life.

It's the same with real estate. They want to make sure that you've flown that plane. You've done that already. Again, if you have it, find a mentor, find a coach, and find a Market pro that will share with you in the beginning to get you going. Set up Google Alerts for your Market you work in so you are on top of new things coming or going on in the area you are a Market Pro in.

How familiar are you with condominium associations? Which associations have no reserves? Which ones get the highest rents? Which ones do not allow rentals? Allows pets? A Market Pro will know this information. In this business, being stupid and not knowing something can cost someone a lot of money and cost you to lose your reputation and possibly your license.

MARKETING

If your advertising looks like an ad, they're not going to look at it. They only care about what's important to them. You really need to make sure that you have to find what their problems are. We're going to go through some actual problems that people have.

We're going to be able to create some of your unique selling propositions that you'll launch too. We're going to recreate what you do, like your marketing plans. Have you ever seen people that have their ads as huge pictures of themselves for real estate and it's just got the little bitty line here that says about the house that they're trying to sell? To me, that is one of the things that you might want to consider not doing. That's all I can say.

Of course we all know the only vote that counts in dealing with you is, who? It's the client. However, I have had to fire a couple of people before, and I will go into that later because we are human beings. We deserve to be treated like human beings. We've all run across that. Let's do this one. Here is an email I sent to someone who was just rude and was yelling at me, slammed the door on the way out and all because I said to her that "The Seller has instructed me to not present any offers that are below 140 thousand dollars". She wanted to offer 130 thousand and she

Marketpros.com

insisted I call him anyway, on a Sunday to boot. My seller was an Investor who owned 100's of properties. I refused to call him and was nice about it and tried my best to explain how things work in the Real Estate business, she was a scientist, a mad scientist that day. LOL. She subsequently went to a Real Estate Professional who she had dealt with before and ended up buying the exact same unit I showed her on Sunday for 140 thousand on Monday. Did I feel like I lost commission?

Absolutely not. I felt grateful, I don't like walking on egg shells. I did not have any stress or didn't have to worry if she was going to be in a good mood or not and that my days going forward were filled with the people who wanted to utilize my time, knowledge and heart.

The second reason I didn't mind not getting the other side of the deal was for the other agent the fact that she has put up with her prior. My thinking was that perhaps this will create some kind of loyalty and respect for this particular Real Estate Professional. Bless her soul. Here is my email it went like this:

Good Morning xxxxxxxx

After thinking about the miscommunication there was toward the end of the time we spent together on Saturday, I feel it is best served for both of us to end any type of relationship. Both of us value our time as an incredibly important part of our day to day life.

I make lifelong relationships with my clients who I work with and my goal is to be as upfront and honest as I can, so they can be educated and informed sharing what I know. My intentions come from a point of serving not just financial gain, to help in order for them to buy or sell that what is in the best interest for them.

I feel you are an incredibly smart and intelligent woman, we just are not aligned and that's Ok, I wish you luck and hope you find another Broker or agent who you can work with to help you accomplish your investment goals.

I appreciated the opportunity.

Thanks,

Kerry Jayne Jackson
Lic. Florida Real Estate Broker
Florida Realty Expertt

FLORIDA REALTY EXPERTS

Most real estate agents never ask their clients for feedback about what they did or didn't like about their process. Even if you have a client that just so happens, because if we all got a 100%, close to a 100% of every single person we dealt with, you wouldn't be reading this right now because you'd be like teaching or on an Island in Fiji somewhere. I have lost customers because of little things that have happened. But I've been able to go back to them.

Say, "Listen, I understand that you didn't buy. I just wonder, could you tell me if there was something that I did along the way?" Just ask them, and then you'll learn more from your mistakes.

And maybe you might not make the same mistakes that I did because I could help you save you on a learning curve.

The biggest things you're going to get in your business are going to be coming from your clients, or people on an airplane, or people that when you're in a conversation sitting down anywhere. Have you ever tried this? I did on a flight from San Diego back to Panama City Beach. They actually wrote down the three things that mattered most to them. On one side, an attorney who said his main concern was someone who knew the area and the covenants and restrictions of the area, 2nd was that the agent's personality be genuine and honest and third was someone who would work around their time schedule. I lost the other napkin or used it, LOL. Organization has never been my strong suit. My friends and family have always been amazed at how I can make so much money and

Marketpros.com

do so many transactions by being so disorganized. I hate to admit that but it is true. In case you want to try it yourself on your next train or plane ride, I would start the conversation like this.

"Oh, I'm a Real Estate Professional. Listen, I'm not trying to sell you a house honest. I'm just always trying to make myself a little bit better. Have you ever bought a house before?" "Yes." And, again do that same scenario, "Do you mind telling me, what was it that you really liked the most about your Real Estate Professional? What was it that you didn't like about them, if there was anything?" Again, that's big, that's really big.

If you can even just take that one suggestion and use that with the people you run into, that's going to add a bit more knowledge to your knowledge base as far as being a Market Pro.

Rule #3 of real estate sales is: You must have your whole heart in your business in order to improve on it. When you do an ad or you do something, try not to get yourself too locked in, so you could gauge to see if that actually works. If it doesn't work, it's okay. You can always create something else. Actually, a lot of times you can learn from other businesses or go to events like the Market Pros one or a Dan Kennedy event. Your best Investment is always yourself first. Invest in courses, seminars, workshops, boot camps or anything that will get you to become better at what you do. Plus, you get to rub elbows with others who are likeminded and can share their ahahs with you.

What Do You Put in Ads?

You have to give them a command on your ads. When you put an ad in the paper, which no is mostly online, they have to do something for a free report. Let me give you an idea. This is a really good listing, if you like listings.

Put out an ad in Facebook or LinkedIn or whatever way you want to do it, at the paper media, mail out, however you want to do it, offering a free report on "How to make your home more valuable with five simple steps." It's a free report.

Just email and you might want to consider not putting your name. This has been a goldmine for me. This is how I get a lot of my leads on my website. I don't put "contact Kerry Jackson". I put, "Please, any information you need to send inquiries askquestions@floridarealtyexperts.com or freereports@floridarealtyexperts.com". They will go to me. But they think it's going to some free report automatic-generated thing that they click on "free report on how to prepare your house for sale" and a free report automatically just flows through to them.

But it does. It comes to me and then I send out a free report automatically through my CRM (Mail Chimp or Infusion soft). Now, I have the name and the information of a person who I know is trying to increase the value of their home because they want to sell it eventually.

You wait a month or however long you want to wait, three weeks. Hopefully, they've done all those repairs and those things that were on the free report you sent them. They are going to make their house more valuable.

Then you send them directly something saying, "Thank you. I hope you enjoyed your free report. Because you took the time to ask for that free report, I'm now giving you a free market analysis that you can use within the next 60 days". Or the next 90 days, or the next 30 days.

With that, now you've got a chance to make a relationship with these people. Because all you've done is just gone to the internet. Right now, you're at the point where you have a name. You can call them, because you have to go to their house to do a CMA. You can't do it just on a computer. You can't do it just over the phone. You have to do it physically.

When you are a professional Real Estate Professional or Market Pro, you actually have to say, "In order for me to give you a good Comparative Market Analysis, I can't do it from just the outside. It wouldn't be fair to you. So, if you don't mind, can we set up a time that I can come and look at the inside of your house just to give you a better idea? It will take me a couple of days longer to prepare the report, and I'll give you an accurate report. No strings attached."

Marketpros.com

They will say, "Yes," because they want it. They want to sell their house. They don't know that they need your help yet because they haven't made that rapport and haven't formed that relationship with you yet. Your heart hasn't hit theirs yet so they don't know that yet.

When you walk in the door, and you have your heart aligned, you've got your habits, your ethics, your attitude, you have that resilience going on, you're going to go in there and gain their trust. Does that make sense? Are you liking this? In the meantime, have you looked them up and found that commonality that will allow you to bond even better with them.

That's a listing right there. I don't know how many people are going to jump at your reports. You can create any kind of reports. But if you get the idea where I'm going with this, it's that if you find something that people need. Then, you're going to be the one that's going to provide the answer for them. It's going to be free.

Again, the secret is not using your name because when you use your name in the beginning, they're going to think, "Oh, it's another real estate salesperson and they're going to try and get my house listed." But if you have a free report at whatever real estate company, they think it's an automated thing. That's my ninja idea for today.

Rule #4 of real estate sales: You need a unique, persuasive, compelling reason to choose you as an agent. Why would you choose you as an agent over anybody else? Think about it.

You have to have something different that you're offering that nobody else does. Every client wants to know, what are you going to give to me? What are you going to help me with? The whole thing is, the biggest thing is you're an expert. A MarketPro

You have a big heart. You have the time for them. Again, the same three things keep coming up, time, knowledge, and heart. Those are the three things you have as a MarketPro.

Don't brag. I would suggest you don't say, "I've been in this industry 15 years. I've won all kinds of awards. I've made $40 million. I'm this, and I'm that. That's why you should pick me. I own my own company. I'm the boss. I'm the broker. So, you ought to pick me to work with."

They don't care. They really do not care. All they want to know is, "I want somebody who can tell me what they're going to be able to do for me." "How can you make my life better" Should I trust you and why? If they know you are a Market Pro, there will be no doubt. Only then can you share your knowledge and experience in the area they are located in while you are letting them know how you are able to help them

Your marketing message that you put out has to be aligned with that. Again, find the problems. Make yourself available to solve that problem.

In a recent event, I had a Broker of 10 years I will share what happened in our conversation. "Pearl, do you have certain problems that you've come across that you want to figure out. What your message might be, that would counteract that problem of people not responding to return emails. Perhaps that you could create a message to go out to some of your clients? Like the people you meet?

Pearl: I actually don't remember the comments, but most of the people that I run to don't even know that I own the company.

Kerry: That's funny you say that. I have a review saying, "I hope your boss knows how valuable you are." I have that email. I thought it was hilarious. I replied, "I'll let her know"

Pearl: Actually, I do make sure to look at their specific needs. I don't tell them how many years I've been in the business. I've never been in on a listing or anything that I haven't gotten.

Kerry: Got it. But we haven't come across what you need yet. We'll go on here. If you try to be an expert on everything, you're not going to be an expert. Pick your niche market or area that you

Marketpros.com

want to go after. Start there. You're always going to sell outside of it from referrals later on.

If you start off as being an expert in a certain niche market whether you want to work with a first-time home buyer. Of course, first-time homebuyers keep your funnel full all the time because you'll never ever run out of first-time home buyers. They're a lot more work. But they're always there because there's not once that I've ever seen that where there wasn't a home buyer program put on by the government.

They're always a 100% financing out there, somewhere for somebody. If not, there's a way to cover their down payment, somehow, some way, some shape, some form. That's a whole other topic that we can go into for people who want to learn how to work with first-time home buyers only.

Do you want to be a Waterfront Specialist? Your USP should say so. You ought to have relationships with local boat dealers, dock and boat lift companies and build those relationships for future referrals.

If you want to do luxury home sales, as I said, every niche market has its own specific message that you need to get across to people. So, pick one of them. Learn it inside out by reading or attending seminars. Again, you'll end up getting WHAT YOU WANT WHEN YOU GIVE ENOUGH PEOPLE WHAT THEY WANT...

I have at one time picked a special niche market. But I ended up doing everything based on referrals. I tried to keep advertising just that niche market. But because I did a good job with what I was doing, it would transfer over, they'd go, "My aunt wants to buy beach home. I know you do first-time home buyers, but can you sell her something on the beach, too?" "Oh, my... let me think. Yes, I can."

Just remember, you're not after everyone. You're only after the ones who you're going to be of value to.

29

Rule #6: It must be easy and fun for the prospect to do business with you.

Again, it comes down to who you want to deal with. If you walk in the room and there was somebody that was a bit of a downer, and you had somebody who was happy and was smiling, who would you rather do business with? That's just common sense.

You must schedule time away from your business, to improve and implement the things that are important to your clients. You have to have time to work on your business. What I call this is infinite time. If you want to write that down, that is really important. Infinite time.

Does anyone know what infinite time means? Do you know what infinite time is? Infinite time is time that-- just say that what you make $120,000 a year. You made $10,000 a month and you divide that into the hours you worked, that's how much you make an hour.

If you actually wanted to double that or triple that, if you actually set up your systems, set up ideas, and spent the time that might be taken away, from you not working in your business, you're working at your business. It might take you 2 days to set up a campaign and gather the information and write all the emails or ads you are doing. If you get 8 sales out of it from people calling you within 2 or 3 days after email is sent out, you are probably going to make a lot more than not doing that. That is a form of infinite time. I learned about Infinite time when I went to an Eric Lofholm Seminar in San Jose back when I first started in Real Estate.

Kevin Harrington and Kerry Jackson at Mastermind in St. Petersburg 2014

Kevin Harrington is the inventor of the infomercial, original Shark on Shark Tank, and Pioneer of the "As Seen On TV" Industry. After hanging around Kevin, as he is part of a Mastermind I belong to, I have learned some valuable tips that have helped me in my business. Although he is not a Real Estate Professional, he is successful in what he does in both Shark Tank and his As Seen on TV. He is always giving, which is another reason to associate with Likeminded People who also live from the inside out on a regular basis. Masterminds are time and money well spent. Success starts from the inside. You are the average of the 5 people you associate with the most.

More on INFINITE TIME

You set-up a program that's going to actually give you non-stop leads but you might spend two or three days doing it, but you say to yourself, "Oh, I can't take away from my business that long." Those three days that you spent working on that follow-up system, entering all the database whether you hire somebody for or you do it yourself, all of that time that you do coming up with your marketing ideas, coming up with the things is going to create that extra money for you down the road. It's going to actually make your income that much larger. My time I spent writing this book, I wasn't getting paid so to speak for the hours while I was writing it, but the book sales and the business that spins off from the book will create more income than had I been paid per hour to write the book. Does that make sense? The time I have spent with 7 Figure speaking Empire over the past 3 years in my spare time, I also consider Infinite time I spent with them while I was creating this Market Pros program and getting my life aligned spiritually as well..

You see all the people in the picture below also played a part of who I have become. I'm certain without the coaching on my speaking, I never would be writing this book and inviting you to my workshops or Bootcamps where I can share all the unique things they don't share with you anywhere else in this Industry.

Marketpros.com

That's your infinite time. That's the time that you can't do without. You've got to take the time to do that. If you don't do that, you're going to get stuck in your business every day. You're going to constantly be answering phone calls and be stuck in your business both mentally and financially. What I might suggest that you could consider doing is to take that time to prepare for the next year and just do and be your best.

That extra 8 to 12 hours you spend on your marketing in setting things up will make you triple or double your income. Is it worth it? It was infinite time that you needed to spend.

Again, it's basically coming up with systems. Systems. Everyone knows what the definition of systems is. What is it? Save Your Self-Time, Energy and Money, The Systems. You can't do everything all by yourself.

When it's only you, you're going to find that you're going to run out of time, money, energy and ideas. Once you've run out of that, what do we have left?

Nothing. Exactly.

33

When you research what an average FULLTIME Real Estate Professional makes, it specifies that **IF** they work over 60 hours a week they average over $87,000 a year. Yet some work 30 hours a week and make $500,000 or more a year in the same area in the same market. Get the picture?

Robert Allen being one of the other key influences in a lot of Real Estate Professionals lives, I was able to spend 2 days at his Mansion with about 15 other people just learning his secrets. He is famous as not only an influential investment advisor, he has authored several bestselling personal finance books including *Multiple Streams of Income*, *Nothing Down*, *Cracking the Millionaire Code, The One-Minute Millionaire: The Enlightened Way to Wealth* (coauthored with Mark Victor Hansen), and *Cash in a Flash: Fast Money in Slow Times* (also coauthored with Mark Victor Hansen). I was fortunate enough to attend one of Roberts series of investment and personal development seminars through his company held at his mansion with a small group of people from all over the world.

He calls his school the Enlightened Wealth Institute. A popular talk-show guest, Robert Allen has appeared on hundreds of programs, including *Good Morning America*, *Your World with Neil Cavuto*, and *Larry King Live*. He has also been featured in *The Wall Street Journal*, *Newsweek*, *Barron's Money Magazine*, and *Reader's*. Oh I forgot to mention he is part of my Mastermind as well.

Marketpros.com

INNER CIRCLE?

Where setting up these systems should help you. There's other ways to what I call is our "Inner Circle". In this business, we have what we call an inner circle. We actually have a board that is our Inner Circle Board.

When our vendors come in, they know that they're in our inner circle. We invite them to be our inner circle.

An inner circle is somebody you can trust. Someone who is likeminded and aligned inside and out. My inner circle right now is helping me to be able to be here for a week, still close deals, still write contracts, and make sure that roofs are put on, termite inspections are done. All those things are looked after.

I have an assistant. However, she relies on the inner circle, as well. If you don't have an inner circle yet, I would suggest you put together one. I'll give you the basics of it. But it's a little more, I actually have a package on inner circle as well. I've got a CD just on inner circle on how important it is and what are the key things.

But basically in my inner circle right now in my company--I have a termite company--I have a surveyor, I have two surveyors. I have a roofer. I have a plumber. I have electrician. I have carpenters and of course attorneys and accountants, flooring people, window guys, cleaners, painters, dry wall hangers and finishers lenders etc.

I have anything that if ever gone wrong with anything in a real estate deal, I have reached out and I have sought out somebody who is aligned with me, who demonstrates that they have a HEART, that they are aligned with their Habits, their Ethics, their Attitude, Resilience and Trust.

You learn from experience who you can trust and who you cannot trust. In this business, sometimes you run across people that you think are aligned and they might not be. But that's okay. You can't expect everyone to be that way, only hope most are.

You can easily eliminate. You can take from the inner circle and put them on the outside of the circle again. Bring in somebody else to your inner circle. But when you're talking to these people,

Marketpros.com

when you're talking to these inner circle people that you've invited in, they know that the reason we're asking you to be part of our inner circle, we would like to give you all of our business, if you're okay with that.

Because we want to know that we can trust you. We want to know that you're going to look after us and our clients no matter what. How we do business is, we jump through hoops for our customers. We're hoping you'll do that for us as well as our customers too.

When you get them meaning the vendors, on track, trust me, they feel special. Everybody feels special when they think that they are part of a team and part of our inner circle. My AC guy Travis, through my Inner Circle he has been exposed to two different developers and is their go to person for a total of 300 plus residences now. Do you think being aligned pays off? You Bet.

Again, find those inner circle people. You probably already have some. Don't you? You have some inner circle people already? Just create your own inner circle. If your company doesn't have an inner circle, ask them if they would help you put one together. Or, maybe you could help them put one together. You can either suggest you have a company one or set up your own private one. Let your clients know they have access to your Inner Circle. People new to the area will consider this so valuable.

It's more beneficial to these inner circle people to have the entire brokerage set one up. Usually, you try to get two of every trade because in this business you can be sued if you refer somebody and they mess up. They go, "My Real Estate Professional, I'm going after her because she makes big bucks. I'm going to go after her because she referred me to this guy." They will sue you, trust me.

So, give them two. Give them two names and tell them to choose from and say, "You can trust these two people. They are in our inner circle."

Did that help at all? Did that make sense? Okay, good. That's leveraging the people around you. That's what that was.

Rule #9 of real estate sales: Stop reinventing the wheel. If you see somebody else's system is working, use it. Just learn it and use it. Systems actually give you a constant flow of income. That's what you want in any business.

Yes, it's great to have a heart and it's great to have good ethics because you'll feel better. But you'll feel even better when you have money to go along with that. Trust me it might not come through that customer; it might show up through another channel.

You need a system that's going to attract customers, convert them to appointments, convert the appointments to clients, and provide the clients with the best service. How do you do it: with your inner circle, people you've already selected that you know do a good job, and you can trust them.

We know we're in a different real estate market than we were 10 to 20 years ago because I had a beeper when I started in real estate, if that tells you anything. I hated to give it up but I did.

We all remember the first phone, the first flip phone, the car phone, and then it was the iPhone. I know I'm behind the times, still. I haven't got a Mac yet. I'm out-of-date, at least that's what my kids tell me.

But the real estate market is not the same. Things change as far as possibilities on how to market yourself. Make sure of new marketing strategies, new overall focus of how you think about your business and where it's going.

A new direction for your business, new energy from your support team, and a new outlook on your marketplace because the market we are going into is a totally different market than where we came from. Totally different.

These people do not want to trust you because they figure the internet is going to protect them. There are many who think the internet is going to help eliminate the need for a Real Estate agent. They really do. Again, it's all about relationships.

If you already have that relationship, they'll trust you way over the internet if you can build that trust. If people from the outside will refer you--the person at the grocery store even refers me-- it's living from the inside out on a regular basis. It really does work when you think about it. Just be out there.

This is an old thing that still works. Do you have a pin? Does anyone have a pin? When you wear your pin, this pin is actually, it cost $10.95 or $14.95. However, this is really like a $45,000 pin. It's not gold. It has no diamonds in it.

But it's a $45,000 pin because that's how much money I've made in commissions from people who noticed my pin in the grocery store, in the gas station, that have said to me, "Oh, does that mean you're a REALTOR?" "Okay." "Oh, good." I'll say, "Can I help you?" And they go, "Yes. I was thinking about buying a house but I don't even know how. I don't know where to start. What do I do?'

"You're talking to the right person." When I go to get gas, I try my best not to do the credit card because no one gets to see you, especially if you're wearing your pin. When you're at the gas station, don't do the card.

Go inside, pay, and talk to the person at the desk. Normally, those are the people who've been working there for a while. They have maybe decided they want to buy a house or whatever that was. You just don't know.

That's where I've met people, like a few at gas stations, one in a grocery store, and they saw my pin. Isn't that crazy? So, wear it all the time if you want to make some more customers. Then, they'll think you're an expert. So get yourself a $45,000 pin.

Of course, we know this business is about building new habits. I've given you a few of them, little ones that I've learned. I'm hoping that what I've told you so far has helped a little bit for some of the habits. Always, always, always, asking and listening, to not just to clients, to everyone. Because there is not one person who has not been affected, impacted, needed, heard of, or been around a Real Estate Professional at any given time.

Now, you're not a Real Estate Professional, John. But, have you ever used a Real Estate Professional? Can I ask you what is the best quality your Real Estate Professional that you can say that's the best quality for the Real Estate Professional you used?

John: He brought a cash buyer, the Real Estate Professional asked because our house wasn't on the market. He had brought somebody that really wanted to pay over what we would have been asking for the house. He was great.

Kerry: What was the quality? If you could name one quality.

John: He reached out to me and said, "Would you be interested in selling your house? I have somebody who wants your house."

Kerry: Okay, I got it.

Basically, what it was, he had a buyer. He went over above and beyond for his buyer. He knew exactly what his buyer wanted. He listened to him properly, I'm sure, because obviously he knew.

There wasn't anything else on the market. He went around the neighborhood and found a house that was exactly what his buyer wanted. He knocked on your door, asked you and said, "I have a cash buyer who wants to buy your house. He's willing to pay you this much. Are you interested?" That's how it went?

That's going over, above, and beyond. That's what we have to do in this business, exactly. He was a good Real Estate Professional. He was proud of it? He had Resilience at that time. The definition of Resilience: capable of withstanding shock without permanent deformation or rupture; tending to recover from or adjust easily to misfortune or change.

During the California Association of Real Estate Professionals conference, Barbara Corcoran said one of the most predominant habits or traits of her top producers had in common, was their ability to pick themselves up and keep going when they experienced a setback.

Marketpros.com

"Not Knowing When the Dawn Will Come, I Open Every Door"

- Emily Dickinson

Inexpensive Techniques for Building your Business

I don't believe anyone was born to be a Real Estate Professional or a Market Pro. When my boys were born, not once did the doctor say, "Congratulations Mr. and Mrs. Jackson, you have just given birth to a healthy 10 pound Real Estate Professional".

This is a difficult career to those who are not aligned properly. Considered one of the most stressful careers in the world.

Becoming a Real Estate Professional is also an expensive proposition for some; I will try to help with that part. I want to commend you because you have made it this far and you are dedicated because you are reading this still. Pick one of the techniques in our system if you are not already loaded with existing clients. Use as much free marketing as you can in the beginning; get some reviews for you and your website. Write blogs and post them on Facebook and LinkedIn. Please make sure you are adding value to someone else. See the video on Adding Value later on Youtube.

Some agents like to make cold calls, knock on doors, sending out mailings... it does not matter which form you end up using, but you must fit this into your daily schedule. Get it done! Don't sit on Facebook all day or even for a couple of hours, put it on your schedule as a task. I have seen agents spend their entire day on their phone scrolling through Facebook and texting back and forth and they wonder why they are not making any headway in the business. If you are sitting at a desk waiting for someone to come to you and Facebook is all you are concentrating on, then perhaps a job doing social media for a Real Estate Professional who does make money might be a better career choice. Some people are just addicted to it. That's OK if that's what you want to do. Just figure out a way to make an income doing it.

Get to know or ask your Broker what they think the best deals are, in the most popular neighborhoods, with the most sales. Then find out who has a listing in this area and pick the busiest, most successful agent and ask them nicely.

"Hi my name is _____ . I am fairly new in the Real Estate industry but I have a lot to offer and wanted to see if I could help you sell your listing in _____ on this street_____? I will set it up; advertise it with both our names on it. Show her a flyer already created. 80% will say yes especially if they are Market Pros. This would benefit their Seller to hold one of these if the Listing agent themselves weren't doing it already. Once you get the green light to do an open house in someone else's listing, now you have the opportunity to get a list of people who come by that you can know add to your database and start a relationship with and so on and so on. A Marketpro doesn't mind helping if they know you are aligned as well.

Marketpros.com

If there was a storm coming or bad weather, you can now call these people and ask if they need any help with anything. I know when a hurricane was coming I would personally call or email my clients who lived out of town and see if I needed to do anything for them to secure their home like putting patio furniture inside for them. You get the picture. Be creative and come from a sense of serving.

If you get it clear when you start that, this is your business. So many agents do not understand that you are the President and CEO of your own company. This is not a job! It is your business, your Lifestyle and it is up to you, if you fail or succeed in order to earn an MBA (Massive Bank Account) in Real Estate. I challenge you to go a whole week and not mention the W word in your vocabulary. When you kiss your significant other or child good-bye, say I am going to list a property, I am going to office to look up something, say anything but that and perhaps it will become a Habit. The word "work" has a negative after effect like someone is forcing you to do it for the money, instead of doing what makes you feel excited and good about being able to help people who need your expertise.

Ads and promotions that worked back in the day when I first started in real estate 17 years ago, 10 years ago, even 5 years ago, they're not working today. I can guarantee you. They're not going to work. We're going to show you later on in the book very soon here within the next couple of pages exactly which ones are working. Like a sprinkler spraying a driveway its only hitting a small percentage instead of the whole lawn. You are wasting money. Right?

"It's tough out there as a Real Estate Professional. We work really hard. We spend a lot of time and money and sometimes that doesn't always work out to make the kind of money we want." That's what non Marketpros say.

What are the rules that we are violating in our business right now, and what are the new rules?

Prospects do not want to be sold. Ever.

- Stop being a real estate salesperson and become a real estate marketer. Become a Market Pro
Salespeople sell clients what they have.
Marketers make sure they have what clients want to buy.
- If your advertising looks like an ad, prospects will tune it right out.
- Prospects only care about what's important to them. They don't really care who you are.
- Make your ads look less like ads and only focus on your prospects.

New Rule #2 of Real Estate Sales
The client has the only vote that counts. Period.
- One of the biggest marketing mistakes real estate agents make is not understanding and addressing client needs.
Most real estate agents NEVER ask their clients for feedback about what they did or didn't like about their process.
- The biggest breakthroughs in your business usually come from your clients, but you must get the information like:
• What motivates the prospects I want to work with?
• What's most important to them about buying or selling a home?
• Do they want a quick sale or the most money?

New Rule #3 of Real Estate Sales
You must test everything in your business in order to improve upon it.
- Instead of guessing, test it out in an ad or on a client and get their feedback. Don't underestimate how powerful this is.
- You must test every component of your marketing pieces. If they don't at least pay for themselves, stop doing it.
- The only way to test something is to require the prospect to take a specific action upon seeing the ad.
- This is called direct response advertising. It allows you to measure and track the effectiveness of all your marketing.

New Rule #4 of Real Estate Sales
Prospects need a unique, persuasive and compelling reason to choose you as their agent.
- Every client always wants to know what's in it for them.
- Don't waste your time with the normal self-promotional and bragging image advertising.

Marketpros.com

- Your marketing message must be specific to your prospects' needs, wants and problems.
- You need a unique selling proposition (USP) that tells customers exactly why they should choose you as their agent.

New Rule #5 of Real Estate Sales
If you try to be an expert on everything, you hinder your effectiveness in everything.
- You must pick a specific type of prospect that you want to target and then tailor all your advertising to that prospect.
- In your real estate business marketing, you should never try to list everything you could do. Pick one.
- You are NOT after ANYone and EVERYone who is looking to buy or sell a home.
- Your ads need to be specific and compelling to draw a specific type of prospect.

New Rule #6 of Real Estate Sales
It must be easy and fun for prospects to do business with you.
- Don't be complicated and difficult, because if prospects have to do too much work, they won't stick around to give you another shot. You need to focus on being inviting, non-threatening, educational, informative and inspiring to do business with.

New Rule #7 of Real Estate Sales
You must take scheduled time away from your business to improve and implement the things that are important to your clients.
- In order for you to view your business from your clients' perspective, you must take time to work on your business.
- Your real estate business is not your life. Your business and your life are completely separate things.
- The key is to step outside your own shoes and become to come up with ways to systemize your standards.
- Your real estate business should serve you and your goals.

New Rule #8 of Real Estate Sales
You can't do everything all by yourself, because it dramatically limits what you're able to accomplish.
- If it's only you, then when you run out of time, money, energy,

ideas, etc..then, there's nothing else. Let us show you how to find affordable assistants.

- Don't fall into the trap of working harder, but getting less and less results. For example, do you close 17 times more deals if you work 17 more hours? No.

- You must leverage your marketing, the people around you and technology to help you make dramatic increases towards your goals and results.

Please don't tell them that you want to sell them something. You want to help them. SHOW THEM YOUR HEART!

I am going to give you some scripts for emails to guarantee that they will return your calls and call you back from an email even if you don't know their names. Look in Back of Book.

You might want to write this down. I put it in the bottom of every single email. In some way, shape or form**,** "I really appreciate the opportunity to help you, find a new beach home or find a new home, relocate you to this area." Whatever it is, "I really appreciate the opportunity to help you," I even if you don't know them yet. You really do appreciate it, don't you? This is free to do.

Wouldn't you say "you do still appreciate it" because they are going to bring you money eventually even though your first thought should always be, "How can I help you?" Zig Ziglar said, "If you help enough people get what they want, you will get what you want."

Again, when I said the year that I made the $30,000 in Real Estate, my first thought that first year in real estate was, guess what? What was I thinking about? Money. I was thinking about money. I was coming from a sense of scarcity instead of from a place of giving and serving. That was why I didn't make any money because every customer I would see or run into, every person I would speak to, the first thing I do is think to myself, "I wonder how much money I'm going to make on this deal. I wonder how much she's going to buy. I wonder what their price range is. I wonder what they're pre-qualified for." I really need to make money.

That was always going through my head. Of course, that was the year I made no money. When I switched my thinking

Marketpros.com

around and confronted everybody, my first thought is, "What do I know that I can help them with?"

I also want to mention that subsequently, I became a volunteer at the school and eventually ended up President of the Booster Club for the entire High School. That volunteer position gave me the knowledge of how Board of Directors conducts business. That lead to me becoming President of the board for a Condo Association with 300 units for almost 3 years which in turn 2 years after I resigned. I was asked to be the exclusive brokerage in that Condo development having my office upfront. Generating over $200,000 in income and still going, I had no idea it was going to lead to me making money when I was volunteering. The leadership I showed on that board got out and I had another developer asked me to be President of the Board for a Townhouse Community in Callaway. This was all volunteer but as I mentioned earlier, I ended up making money but it came from a different channel later on with many referrals. Later on in the book, you will read how this is called connecting the dots backwards.

This is me in Miniature Village in Toronto Canada in 1965.

Who would have figured.

How many times have you heard people say, "It's a custom of ours, or I have a tendency to do, That's so characteristic of me or I've used this one, I have a tendency to or that's just my style".

47

In reality, this just means you have habits no pussy footing around with these clichés. Whether they are, good or bad, it is your decision. I am just going to share what successful Real Estate Professionals who are successful and happy with their lives have in common when it comes to Habits. You can wake up and say, "How many new friends am I going to be able to meet today that I can help with what I am good at or you can say I have to go to work and make some money". Your mindset will be totally different from one to the other.

You can decide to be successful or unsuccessful or to be lazy or productive sounds like Good or Bad which to me it is. Bad Habits cannot only interrupt your life and your business relationships, they will sabotage your life by preventing you from accomplishing your goals, they also jeopardize your mental and your physical health, bad habits waste precious time and energy.

When I decided at 52 years old I wanted to become a Speaker and speak about my message, I wanted to do something else with my life that gave me the flexibility to travel and make a living at the same time. I had no idea how difficult it was going to be. But I had reasons, which as I said earlier don't count though. It didn't matter I had no extra money as I was in the middle of a lawsuit that had been going on for 3 years, my mom who was my best friend died, I had to make sure my boys were ok, I had to spend time visiting my dad because of his loss. I had to run a business and deal with an alcoholic husband and the fact I had bill collectors from 17 mortgages crawling up my skirt. But as I said earlier if I continued to say why I wasn't moving forward, those reasons would never give me the results I have today and besides Robert Schuler said "Reasons don't count, its Results that count.

How many people have had a goal, how many have had a goal and failed to achieve it, but wanted to give reasons why and kept their story going, telling everyone they ran into and using it as the reason they couldn't move forward or complete something.

I looked at what was taking up all my time, I wanted a solution and when you want something bad enough you will find a solution to get the result you want. But why couldn't I find time to work on my goal, so I looked at the things I did every day that took up time that wasn't helping me go in a forward direction. "I made some mistakes that have put me where I am right now. The blessing in this was that once you have become a Market Pro in Real Estate, you will always be one. You can take that at any age to any area and make money if you want to or have to.

Although Jim Rohn said "Make measurable progress in reasonable time, I wasn't sure what reasonable was so I kept trying and discovered."

It was my little habits, like reading the newspaper from cover to cover every morning, I freed up at least an hour. I then gave up a phone call from someone who liked to call every morning just to gossip about everyone else, that added 30 minutes of wasted time, plus put my state of mind in a bad place for sure. I told her our morning chats would have to be put off until I achieved my goals as I needed every minute to get me there, I had a lot of catching up to do seeing I was starting over from scratch, that is in the financial end of things only?

Watching the news after work and the same news at 10:00 p.m. That was another 2 hours. That's not including wasting time at work talking about the news, something that has nothing to do with me and there was nothing I could do about it. If there was something that was happening in the news that was going to be beneficial to my clients or prospective clients, then I would have an email from Google as I have set up Google alerts for anything like that. That's over a 100 hours a month, 50 days a year I was wasting and you can learn to do a lot of things with 50 hours. This goes along with the quote by Gandhi "Live as if you were to die tomorrow and Learn as if you were to live forever."

Sometimes you have to change your environment to change a habit sometimes, if you want to quit drinking, stop going to the local bar, that's obvious right? You just can't do that. In Real Estate we all have habits, some good and some not as good. I had this habit of giving my opinion when it wasn't asked for yet.

To break a bad habit, you need to replace it with a good one. Motivation won't work because it's temporary. Zig Ziglar quote says it best, "People often say that motivation doesn't last. Well, neither does bathing - that's why we recommend it daily.

So the only way you can change is to change the behavior. Don't design it by the outcome, design it by the things you have to do to get to the outcome. Your habit is to do it a little bit at a time and systematically don't look at the effort.

I used to look at my boys and shutter sometimes, although they were straight A students, they spent 3-5 hours a day playing games or watching TV or sports on the TV or their Kindle. One of them has figured out that when I said you only have one chance at life there is no re dos, is really a true statement. I am certain the other ones' habits will change as he gets older. It takes a desire to change a habit

It sounds like the news was my worst habit, I don't consider drinking wine with my dinner a bad habit yet. What habit is taking hours away from the things you really want to do.

"Most people do not listen with the intent to understand; they listen with the intent to reply."

Stephen R. Covey
(1932-2012)

Marketpros.com

Habit # 1: LISTENING

What is it that make successful sales people succeed. "Ralph Nichols once said the most basic of all human needs is the need to understand and be understood. The best way to understand them is to LISTEN"

Listening is a learned thing, when you are not a good listener you miss opportunities that will help you. Most people think they are good listeners, very few people think they need to develop their listening skills, but in reality, very few people can really be effective listeners and it's not because it's difficult or too hard, it's because most of us never developed the habit of becoming an effective Listener. Listening creates Trust, it gives you so much knowledge and insight because you get so much information from someone, you know what motivates them, what they need, are you seeing where sales people really need to hone in on that Listening habit. —

Lee Lacocca, Former CEO Chrysler Corporation:

"*I only wish I could find an institute that teaches people how to listen. Real Estate agents need to listen at least as much as they need to talk. Too many of them fail to realize that real communication goes in both directions.*"

Because there are people, myself included sometimes, that when someone is speaking, instead of listening to what is being said, I am already listening in my head of what I am going to say. Especially when you know they are going around the room and asking people to say something or share something, I slip sometimes and do this I really do try to focus on what the other person is saying. I want to tell you when I realized I had a listening problem and why I really started trying to make this a habit.

This was a time after the storm as Les would say. I was in a conference room with Les Brown above in picture and a few others who were also being mentored by Les and Julie.

They recorded the sessions so we could listen to ourselves and remember Les Brown's advice. While I was listening on the way home from Orlando, I noticed where I jumped into conversations and gave advice, I listened to our Wed coaching calls that were recorded and I noticed I tended to do the same thing.

I was recently out with a customer and I recorded our conversation, not for YouTube or anything other than to see if I was learning to listen. It was amazing how much you learn about yourself when you are recorded and/or videotaped during day-to-day events, that's why reality TV is so raw.

When I do fall off the wagon so to speak, it's normally when I want to give advice to someone who hasn't asked for it and

Marketpros.com

for that matter probably doesn't want it. But I am such a giving person, with a big mouth sometimes I would go ahead and give unsolicited advice, you know telling them what they should do and how to do it. I said I was just Type A.

That's how a lot of disagreements begin in relationships and how you can turn away customers inadvertently. When you are telling someone what to do, you are dominating the conversation and you are not listening.

Someone once told me, "I bet your ears have never got you in trouble before".

Of course, if you have read the Inner Voice by Russ Whitney you know that is not the way to do it.

If you have actually been through something similar yourself to that situation, then use an example of what happened to you and how you overcame it or handled it or were defeated by it, whatever the truth is. Otherwise, just listen and if they ask for advice then go ahead. Calvin Coolidge said, "no one ever listened their way out of a job", you can say the same thing about sales"

Many people have commented on Listening,

— Diane Sawyer ABC Television Anchor said

"*I think the one lesson I have learned is that there is no substitute for paying attention.*"

You know our brains have a lot of capacity. We can think 4 times the speed of a speaker speaking, so you have time to reflect and say it back to them, don't be like a parrot though, say it as you understood it.

— Stephen R. Covey who wrote *7 Habits of Highly Effective People* said,

"Seek first to understand, then to be understood."

Or as Robert Schuller says "*Big Egos have little ears*"

"To say that a person feels listened to, means a lot more than just their ideas get heard. It's a sign of respect. It makes people feel valued."

Such a simple thing, listen with your Heart and keep practicing to where it becomes a Habit, make your customers feel valued your friends and coworkers too.

HABIT #2 : BE GIVING

I could have just said giving, but as I said in the beginning, this is not what you have, it's who you are. This is another part of living with the Heart method or from the inside out. Practice pro social behaviors, I guarantee you it moves us from helplessness to helpfulness.

Visionary and Author of E Myth, Michael Gerber and I in

St. Petersburg after a dinner with fellow Speakers and Entrepreneurs.

Michael Gerber's E-Myth Point of View embodies his commitment to personal growth and the realization that a business owner's purpose in life can be actualized through his or her business. Michael Gerber's efforts, his message--his very life's work has been to empower business owners to gain more freedom, more money, more time, and more life.

HABIT #3: *Finding Solutions, Not Excuses*

Robert Schuler once said there are only 2 things in life: Reasons and Results and reasons don't count.

How many of you have had a surprise you weren't expecting ....? I call that a problem ...... I have a Habit of looking for a solution to any problem. Because a problem is something you can do something about. If you can't do something about it, then it's not a problem. It's a predicament. How true is this statement? How many times do we allow a problem to become a predicament? Most likely, more times than we want to admit. Sometimes if we have a problem, we try to avoid the circumstances causing the issue. When, in fact, all we are doing is making the problem into a predicament, almost unsolvable, almost too large to handle. What we have to remember is that every problem has a solution. We may not like the outcome, but there is a solution. In Real Estate, a problem might be you can't get into a place because there are renters and the other agent said, "sorry they won't let us in". I have had that happen and I have also been able to get in eventually, might have to buy a gift card for them to go out for dinner or a Starbucks gift card in exchange for 10 minutes or so to look. I have actually paid a housekeeper to go clean for a renter so they weren't embarrassed when they said "Oh I haven't had time to clean up so I don't want anyone coming over". Find out what that thing is they would be willing to trade for you to be able to look. They know that should your Buyer buy, it might mean they have to move. I always reassure people in that situation that I will help them if they call me.

When we have problems, they serve as reminders that we cannot succeed alone and they also can be huge opportunities for us and others. We need help on occasions and that help comes from others. Maybe others with experience in the area we are failing. We should reach out to others who have had similar experiences and allow them to guide us and teach us through the issue we are facing. We have to become humble and teachable in those moments. Did anyone ever say to you "You are who you associate with". I like to say that you are the average of the five people you associate with the most. Sometimes, that is your problem. When we have problems, they provide opportunities to pull us out of ruts and allow

Marketpros.com

us to think creatively. We cause some of our problems by continuing to do the same old things, the same old way and we get in a rut. What is good about a rut is it is open on both ends to allow us to exit. We do this with creative thinking, thinking outside of the "Rut". There are other ways and opportunities to resolve the problem; we just have to think differently.

I would say part of my success in Real Estate was to do that. I have had many times I have had to many things that a lot Real Estate Professionals or Real Estate Agents wouldn't do. A Market Pro would though because they have had those experiences or been around long enough. An example of one that nobody thought would close was a Motel that the Buyer actually called me and said he knew what he wanted but was having a hard time convincing the Seller to sell to him. He was wishy washy. I developed a relationship with the Seller, first visit was strictly I said to him "I want to get to know you and find out if you really do want to sell your motel". I think he thought I was crazy, but in reality, my time is valuable like everyone else's and determining if I could help would determine his motivation for selling. After speaking to him, it came out that he had grand children who were 7 and 10 years old and he had seen them 12 times, period in their life.

I knew then I could make this work although he had a strong emotional hold on a business he had owned for 25 years, I believed that the grandchildren thing was going to be the determining factor. Every time I presented him with the offer (four or five tries) over a 4-month period, he would come up with a different reason why he wasn't going to sign. First, it was "I need another month or two to look over my files and get them out of the motel". We told him he could stay for free for a month. Then it was when his attorney was out of town and he wanted him to give him his blessing on the sale. We found him a different attorney and recommended he speak to him. He did.

Then he said he hired a new manager and committed to him that he would be there 90 days. The Buyer agreed to meet him and liked him and agreed to keep him on. Then he was going to have to pay too much taxes. So I asked the Buyer if he would raise the price enough to cover his taxes of 120k. Reluctantly he did. There were some other things that came up the day before closing and the day of. It was one obstacle after the other. We closed and everyone was happy about 5 months after we started.

Just FYI, my first phone call I had with the Seller which was "I don't want to deal with Real Estate Professionals and I am not paying a Real Estate Professional fee". Funny, I never once thought "I don't think I will be able to make this work." I kept the conversation like this to myself and the buyers and kept that thought in my head and heart every time I spoke to the seller. I just kept thinking of how much he will enjoy his grandchildren now, I also reminded him of that. Sometimes we are so busy we can't see outside the box because we don't take the time to look. I did mention to him in our conversations about a book I had recently read (another Good Habit) how when interviewed, some older individuals nearing the end of their life were questioned and asked if they would have done things differently what would they have done. There were a few answers that most everyone said the same thing. One was that they wouldn't have worked as much or spent too much time making a living instead of building a life. We have the opportunity to make friends and make this a lifestyle instead of the W word or J word I talked about earlier.

This says it all. A Market Pro looks at their experiences in the Real Estate Industry like this

Don't regret knowing the People who come into your life. Good People Give You Happiness. Bad Ones give you experience. The Worst Ones give you lessons. The Best Ones give you Memories.

The Best Memories with one of my clients. The Breelings who have been so giving and generous with their wisdom and knowledge. They were there for me emotionally when I needed help getting through a storm.

Marketplos.com

    I met them from a phone call in 2012; they were calling Brokers asking who would give them a 50% referral fee on a condo as their son-in-law was a Real Estate Professional in Colorado and they were moving from Nebraska. I guess I was the only one who agreed to do that. That decision to help them has proven to be a factor that has generated me way more income than I gave up. It has also created a friendship over the last 4 years that will hopefully last a lifetime. They are a couple who have a motto that they have to do something fun every day. They have been an inspiration to me as much as I have been to them at times I hope.

Habit # 4: FORGIVING

Some say Forgiving means remembering without Anger. Just don't hold resentments as "Bitterness is like a poison and you are the container holding it " Think about that one.

How many times have you been upset at another agent because you think he or she stole your listing or your sale? What really happened? Figure out what happened on the other end, what the reason was and learn from it. No one steals anything, except burglars and bank robbers and criminals. If another agent tied up your customer and took them away, it would be called maybe that, but that does not happen. When you lose a client and trust me over the years, I have dropped the ball when I got so busy or didn't have my Inner Circle in place or I didn't follow up and I lost a few myself. Guess what though as much as I wanted to be mad at the other agent who took the client, if I had done what I know now, none of that would have happened. I offer to help them and give them the info I had discovered that they might not know. I actually have clients that say they will wait until I get home if I am out of town. Very important to learn to forgive all agents regardless of how bad they are, as you never know when you are going to have to work with them on the other side of a deal and you also don't want to feel uncomfortable or stressed that you have to talk to them. Plus you are living from the inside out all the time. More so, imagine another agent can't stand you for some reason, the agent sees a listing with your name on it, are they going to send to their client or not? We all know that is not supposed to happen but in reality, there are some agents that behave like that and unfortunately, not all of the agents out there are operating from the inside out. Hence, why sometimes we have been given a Used Car salesman label. It's amazing the number of people who don't trust a Real Estate Professional or Real estate agent. A Market Pro will be associated with the word HEART which ends with Trust. That is my mission.

Reviewing Your 3 Most Important Giveaways to your Clients

Marketpros.com

TIME, KNOWLEDGE AND HEART

> **Time is the greatest gift you can give to someone. Because, it's like giving a portion of your life that you'll never get back.**

Clients appreciate when you truly give them your time.

But the time aspect of it is when you first start, when you're trying to build, you're going to put more time into it. You're going to give potential clients your time but you're going to give it to them on a basis where you're more listening instead of hearing. Not answering text messages as they talk, that is just rude in this Industry.

Reasons Why People Do Not Like Their Real Estate Professionals:

1. The Salesperson fell down on the job.

2. They hate the fact that the Real Estate Professional doesn't take the time to listen to what they want. It's, "Hi, how are you, come into my office or else I don't have time for you." Then the customer is taken on a home tour to see homes that only barely fit their criteria.

3. The agent was just too high-powered, only interested in their real estate for sale (not what the buyers wanted).

4. People get upset that agents rarely follow up when they are more than ready to buy a home. No follow up system.

In Summary --
1) Buyers want to be treated properly.
2) Buyers want to give out the simplest information about themselves.
3) Buyers want an agent who listens, not attacks.
4) Buyers want to deal with positive, friendly agents.
5) Buyers want to be able to look and ask questions without feeling pressured to make a commitment.
6) Buyers want to see what is advertised. If the advertised home has been sold, there should be some others available both more expensive and less expensive, or it looks like the ad has been misleading.
7) Buyers want to create a short list of homes they like through a process of elimination.
Wonder if you are the right agent? Can your Clients answer Yes to all 7?

*The above was based on 2,000 surveys and countless focus groups, as reported by the Los Angeles Times

Listening???

YIKES I have 2 boys that I made a mistake when they were younger and I'd say, "Do you hear me? Did you hear me?" I should have been saying, "Are you listening?" because listening is so much more important, especially in this business. Yet, a lot of Real Estate Professionals only hear and some only hear what they want to hear. Here is a line from a NAR newsletter. "NAR's research has revealed that many consumers experience anxiety afraid to fire their agent once they realize they don't want to work with them"

I'm finding that a lot of times when you're speaking to somebody, I even catch myself thinking of what my answer is going to be to the other person before I've even finished listening to what they have to say. You know what I'm talking about?

Marketpros.com

A good example is if you're passing the microphone, or you're going around the room, you tell somebody, "I want you to give me 30 seconds about yourself." While he is explaining to himself, while he's talking, you are already thinking, "What am I going to say?" At the back of your head, you're going, "Okay," people do that with their customers. Asking them what they really want and while they are talking, they are thinking of how much commission they might be able to make.

If you can just take that example, they know when you're listening to them. I talked to customers, they go, "I know, when I'm speaking, that you really cared. You're listening to exactly what I said." It's hard to sometimes focus because there are other things going on. So when you're giving them your time, think of that as one of the things that you do.

Of course, the second thing is knowledge because you have your time, your knowledge and your heart. Your knowledge is absolutely huge. I'm sitting on an airplane, coming back from San Diego. I had two flights, thank Goodness because I got to survey two people which I like to do a lot.

I always say to people, "I'm a real estate broker. Have you ever bought a house before? I'm not trying to sell you a house. I just want to know, what your best experience was with a Real Estate Professional and what your worst experience was with a Real Estate Professional." I learn from those things. I also use those stories for 3rd party stories that help a client understand better which I will explain in a later chapter.

Everybody you come across if you were in a conversation with them, ask them. It's not going to hurt you to ask them those questions. It's going to help you. People love to talk about their experiences anyway. People love to talk about themselves. It's just part of human nature. That would be one of the things that can help you gain knowledge.

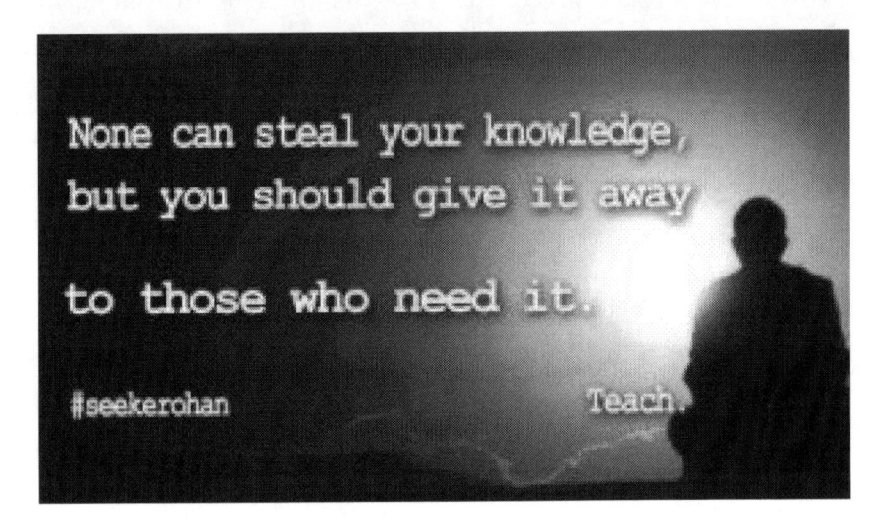

> None can steal your knowledge, but you should give it away to those who need it.
>
> #seekerohan — Teach.

KNOWLEDGE

The other thing is to know your area. If you don't know your area then it's really a little more difficult to sell. If you're new to an area, which Terry here is brand new to an area. She just moved here to Florida from Wisconsin. For her to start in real estate, it is challenging but it can be done. You'll learn later how she can turn her first sale into multiple sales because of how she is using your heart, her knowledge, and her time. She starts out with her Heart, because she's new.

Her heart method first, then her time, and then her knowledge is coming. It's getting there. But knowledge is so crucial because that's the second most important thing that people ask for is, "how well do you know the area"?

If you're not familiar with the area, have a partner. Find somebody to be a mentor that knows the area like the back of her hand. Then, you can honestly say, "We know the area, really, really well. We are experts here. I can tell you anything about any of the condos, any of the homes, any of these subdivisions because we know."

Marketpros.com

Then, you run to your person that's your mentor or your partner and ask them to help you. If you're working in an organization or real estate company that they're not willing to share, then you're probably not in the right company. That's just my suggestion. I shouldn't be so demanding. I've got to learn to instead of saying "You need this..." it should be, "You might want to consider." However, in my opinion.

Of course, the last one is heart. I just wanted to give you an idea of where I'm coming from, what I'm all about, and what has helped me become a Market Pro.

I consider myself an expert in my area. I give the time when I'm there to my customers. I really feel I've learned how to live from the inside out and think about things before I open my mouth most of the time. How you think is sometimes how it ends up turning out. It happens. Try it.

The secret to guaranteeing that your prospects are beating a path to your door. Wouldn't it be nice that you woke up in the morning, you open your computer, and you had ten leads sitting there saying, "Please help me? I need you."

The economy has changed. As I said, we are in a different type of economy. Sellers are more skeptical. Buyers are leery to sign with anybody because they think they're going to be able to do everything over the internet or they think they won't be able to Trust you. They want to make sure that they're making the right decision with you. (Bloomberg) Studies have revealed that over 50% of Buyers can find their own home over the Internet. They interview agents over the Internet through email and use reviews.

But again, if they trust you already, and you've already developed that relationship with them, this won't happen. Just be Authentic.

Definition of AUTHENTIC. Conforming to reality and therefore worthy of trust, reliance, or belief.

Means the things you say and do. Authenticity is not very common these days but when it is there, it shines through your words and actions and is very powerful for creating bonds with others.

Oprah Winfrey said, "I had no idea that being your AUTHENTIC self could make me as rich as I have become. If I had known, I'd have done it a lot earlier."

Being Authentic is so important in this business and I feel I can contribute that as well to my success.

REVIEW OF HABITS FOR SUCCESSFUL MARKET PROS AND HOW YOUR HABITS DETERMINE YOUR FUTURE

1. You Should Have Goals or Dreams, Actually both. You need to write a list for yourself and hold yourself accountable for those goals. I say write it down, not type it on your phone or your laptop. Here's more proof and a decent book I have read, titled "Write It Down Make It Happen – Knowing What You Want and Getting It" by Henriette A. Klauser. It is a collection of stories. Different people who wrote down what they wanted and got it.

Make a goal board or some call it their Dream Line. Whatever you call it, just do it. Put it in your office or wherever you spend the most time. Have both short term and long-term goals. Goals are a good thing regardless of what they are! They help. This will give you your Purpose or even better knowing where you are going. They are dreams with a deadline. I have a picture of a Yacht on my Dream board.

2. Your Record Keeping System will need to track your sales, expenses, and your lead generation   You should track which marketing is working and what is not. You should be able to track and record all of your leads. If you are not as good at this right now, take the time to make yourself into a better organizer. It took me 10 years to figure out I should keep track of my clients; thank goodness a vast majority kept up with me which allowed me to make 6 figures a year on a regular basis. I can't imagine what

would've happened had I kept a system where they automatically got a hello and or Happy Birthday with a message that added some value to their day. It would have been triple that. Mail Chimp is free for sending out these messages. I sometimes just send a motivational letter about life in general something I have learned. In the back of this book are the things I wrote and emailed to everyone in my database. As a Market Pro you get them monthly.

You Should Have Systems. You should automate your business. You need systems for working with buyers, sellers, FSBO's, Expired's, and for your staff, if you have a team. However, pick one system and make it your own. Do not worry if it is perfect at the beginning as long as you start. Just implement, and tweak it along the way until it works.

HAVING GRATITUDE

"We tend to forget that happiness doesn't come as a result of getting something we don't have, but rather of recognizing and appreciating what we do have." - Frederick Keonig

For years, I read about the importance of gratitude but never fully applied it. I thought, "How can being thankful really change my life?" I learned a lot about this through my Mentors and Mastermind especially Dave Van Hoose who was the founder of Foreclosures daily and a Top Speaker and Speaker trainer who I had the privilege of training with. I realized some of the most successful people in the world practice Gratitude.

RALPH WALDO EMERSON says, "Cultivate the habit of being grateful for every good thing that comes to you, and to give thanks continuously. And because all things have contributed to your advancement, you should include all things in your gratitude."

It too becomes a Habit. There are down days for everyone but only for a minute because once you totally are in the Gratitude groove (that's what I call it), things just seem better. Better for your mental and physical health and for all the people who cross your path.

Here is an article from the Huffington Post. I hope they don't mind I put it in my book. This is the best article I have read on Gratitude and I didn't want to be arrested for copyright infringements. So go online CLICK and read this.

http://www.huffingtonpost.com/2014/11/25/everyday-gratitude-practices_n_6212270.html

Managing FEAR

You must manage your inner voice and manage your fears. This is one of the most important elements. Once again, this is another area where you use your Heart Method. They say on the other side of Fear is what you want. EXCEPT in Real Estate, as this is an occupation where people can blame you for things you didn't do. How do I know? I was a target for a lawsuit when the Market crashed in 2008. A past client and his group decided they needed a scape goat for their inexperience and foolish waste of funds they had received from the Federal Government a year prior. A quick version of this Court Battle took over 4 years from the onset, in which I prevailed in local court, Florida Court of Appeals and Supreme Court. Real Estate Professionals have to be so careful and cross their t's and dot their i's and do the right thing all the time. I like to send emails recapping conversations now since this has happened, just to make sure they totally understood what you said and vice versa. It's a must with most people.

We are going to make mistakes, but in this Industry, it costs you. Not as much as Physicians but we are right up there with doctors as far as a few things other than that. We get called all hours of Day and Night similar to doctors'. We see a lot of different people with a lot of different personalities and we have to remember a lot of details about what each person wants. We are capable of making the same amount of money as a doctor. This is why being a Market Pro is so essential.

DRESS how you want to be addressed

DRESS FOR SUCCESS

Dress for Success Being Professional in Dress and Behavior makes you feel more like the Professional that you are. You can still be Different. Did you ever notice that all real estate agents walk and talk the same? When you are different, buyers and sellers will take notice. Always dress one step above the professional you really want to be.

Always look neat. It sounds so simple yet I have seen Real Estate agents and Brokers with greasy hair or they smell like an ashtray or a smelly sock. If you want to be considered a

Professional, a Market Pro, you need to also dress like one, act like one and just be one, all the time.

      Your vehicle is part of the Dress for Success chapter. I recently showed up at a closing and the car next to mine had an agent's magnet on the doors and inside, all I could see was fast food containers, empty cups and just trash all over the back seat. The car was filthy dirty on the outside as well. I don't care how old your car is or how new it is, you can and should always keep it clean. Car washes are a tax deduction I think. I would not even consider using someone for anything if I thought I had to ride in a trashy car. This is the difference between Market Pros and successful agents versus those that don't know yet how to be truly successful. It is such an easy thing too. Would you deal with someone whose car looked like this? I know it's a little extreme but hopefully you get the point. I have actually seen a car like that with a big magnet of a prominent Real Estate Company.

Marketpros.com

Another Habit Important in the Real Estate business I suppose is THINKING OUTSIDE THE BOX.

You must think "Outside the Box" or "Build a New Box" if you can be different and have a USP (unique selling proposition). See Hundreds of examples in back pages to help you create yours. What makes you unique? It is more than being ethical, professional, or trustworthy. What is different about your marketing or the services you provide that will create a Value to clients. Go through the list provided to get you thinking. One of mine is "Dedicated to Results"

You are a Great Human Being and then you become a Marketing expert to become a Real Estate Professional to become a Market Pro. Always be marketing yourself, your business, and your listings to ensure future business. It is not only new prospects but existing relationships of clients you have already worked with. One of your major jobs is marketing for a seller. However, just because you are great at marketing you still need to be a great Real Estate Professional, you still need to know how to negotiate, communicate, and educate using your Heart Methods over and over again. If you think about it how much easier is it to go back to your previous clients? If you have left them with a good feeling because you put your Heart in it when you dealt with them, they will remember, I guarantee it.

Having a Website that Generates Leads- Majority of agent's websites are glorified business cards or even worst, an extension of their brokers website. According to the NAR study, 75% of the top 16% that earn over $100,000 per year have a website. According to studies, Internet Real Estate Professionals or agents have been known to make four times as much income as traditional agents. You need a website that offers information to the consumer, you need to give them value, show them things they don't already know. The sole purpose should be to capture leads. Brand yourself, Content is for your Blog, go onto Active Rain and copy your blogs there as well. Be a marketing agent!

While sinking too much time into tasks like posting on social media and checking junk emails tends to reduce the average agent's likelihood of being happy with their career, there are no diminishing happiness returns for spending many hours on important tasks like following up with leads and attending client appointments.

You should subscribe to internet lead generating companies like Zillow and Trulia when you know you have mastered the Time Knowledge and Heart aspects of being a Real Estate Professional. Yes, I said it, you should pay for leads! 90% of Buyers start their search online and Zillow is well known, more than you perhaps. LOL.

All other companies out there I have tried and wasted my money testing them for you. If you come across a new one, look carefully at their reviews and ask for names of agents to call and verify. Read the fine print on Homes.com

Some agents will say that they never will pay for leads. I do not care how you get your leads; you pay for them already! From relocation companies to ads in the newspaper, you pay for leads. You paid someone to do your website etc. It is important so I am mentioning it again. Studies say that 90% of people buying a home start their search online.

However, with internet leads, there is a way to minimize the costs once you develop a lead generating website and learn how to market your website to consumers. You can build your own campaigns on sites such as Craigslist and drive prospects back to your website. Once you have 100 people as regular referral partners, then you can stop paying for leads.

IF YOU WANT SOMETHING YOU'VE NEVER HAD, THEN YOU'VE GOT TO DO SOMETHING YOU'VE NEVER DONE.

Marketpros.com

SOCIAL MEDIA

This is the social revolution. You should have both a fan page and personal page on Facebook. You should keep your business and personal life separate, but use your personal page to connect with your clients using soft real estate messages. Pick one or two social media platforms and incorporate them into your business. However, do not let social networking run your life or business. I have recently have seen many agents become addicted to social media sites, and many forget about actually generating business. Social media can be a black hole if you are not careful! Do not let friends in a bar post a picture of you or tag you. In your Fan page, post things on real estate related stuff, food, sports and weather. Sounds simple but stay away from Politics and Religion and how much you can drink.

Video is the newest way to advertise yourself. Video should be used for your listings, client testimonials, or to educate your target audience about your services and real estate. YouTube or put videos in emails as well. Google has changed how they move sites to the top of the list and uploading videos is the newest best way to get noticed.

Find some free niche marketing such as Lowe's Real Estate Professional Benefits. Referrals are very important to growing your business. Breakthroughbroker.com provides free newsletter templates to start a newsletter.

You should hire an assistant- Hire an assistant that truly understands what you are looking for. Assistants should help you grow your business. Assistants should free up your time so you can attend to money making activities and hold down the fort to let you go to conferences that will help you grow your business and give you a few days to step outside the lifestyle you have created as everyone needs to refuel or they will break down on the road just like a car that runs out of gas. This is better than splitting your commissions at this point. Get 2 assistants unless you want to take lots of vacations then you need a Real Estate Professional who is aligned with you and thinks with their Heart like you, another Market Pro.

CONVERTING LEADS, CREATING RELATIONSHIPS

Real Estate is the Most Relationship Based Business at any Price level.

In order to convert leads, create a relationship with the person on the other end of the conversation whether it be on the phone or in an email or in line at the grocery store or airport. If you're not thinking HOW CAN I SERVE YOU, this would be your first indicator you will not be able to convert this lead. Now we have established that the second thing is to find some commonality. You must be sincere and genuine. People can read you if you are smiling over the phone or not. Robert Drake who helped come up with the Market Pros idea used to run a mortgage company with over a hundred originators and he bought mirrors for all of them so they remembered to smile while they were on the phone or show true concern. You need to handle objections from both buyers and sellers. It has been said objections are buying signals. You need to learn scripts from others who have it nailed down. Consult with a Market Pro, take theirs but make them your own.

Clients do not like to be "Sold", so do not sound scripted. They want to be helped. If you know how to handle objections and truly have the conversation knowing the reason you are speaking to this customer is because they need your help and you are more than willing to help them with what you do know about your area. Your conversion rates will increase. In our Market Pros semi-annual boot camp, you get real life situations where Real Estate Professionals compete on who worked it out the best. Lots of fun.

If you are living from the inside out, you will be consistent in all your approaches. The real you will come out and this person inside you just does the right thing.

Hire people to do what you don't do well and anything that takes you more than twice the time it should take you. I use a company called Brokers Break that takes all my listing photos and more. My clients love it. Go to BrokersBreak.com to see all the things they do that will allow you to cover more leads, instead of doing time consuming items that you are not a Pro at. It is my son Brady's business, it happened because I could not find someone to

Marketpros.com

do this and realized I could help a lot more people if I wasn't doing the things he likes to do and is good at.

GETTING LISTINGS

Prepare at least 20 listing presentations or however many you want in a certain period.

You must have a Set Listing Presentation That You Follow if you want Listings of course- You need to have a road map that you follow each time.

Always be professional even if it is your best friend, referral, etc. Real estate is not always easy, and you need to be a Pro in your market and have a set listing presentation that keeps the seller on tract from the beginning to the end. Be in control! Be a Market Pro.

You Must Have a Pre-Listing Package for Sellers- A pre-listing package shows that you are organized. It also separates you from other agents. Most agents do not have a pre-listing package that they email or mail before the listing presentation. I like to send the listing package and then follow up with a phone call to see if they received it prior to your visit. This will also cut down on the amount of time you spend on the listing presentation so you can focus on the client and not on your services. This is where your knowledge really helps as you have to be a Market Pro in that area to be successful at not only pricing but marketing a listing for someone.

FOLLOW UP SECRETS

You Must Have Great Follow-up- If you are working with Internet leads, you need to follow up immediately or within 20 minutes or less to be truly successful. You must follow up with all other leads within the hour. Honestly the sooner the better. For every minute that goes by, your chances go down by a percentage. You will end up keeping them for the long haul the quicker you reply. A lot easier to form a relationship with someone when they say, "Wow that was service, you called me back so quickly, thank you". That is what you get when you do. I always answer with,

"This is what I do for a living and I take it seriously, I see you are calling from (wherever it says on your cell phone) and either say, "How is the weather there?" or "I have an uncle (be truthful) or a friend who lives there", and find that commonality right off the bat with them to start the relationship. The next words out of your mouth might be "What can I do to help you?"

Another secret is that when I happened to miss a call I was never afraid to go ahead and call people even if it was a few days later, just in case they haven't tried anyone else and to let them know you felt bad that you missed it or was out of town, whatever the truth is. Worst case is they found someone else. Next say, "I am so glad someone was able to help you". There have been a couple of times I heard "I'm glad you called the other agent didn't know the area at all and was not able to help me". Sad but true. Hence, Market Pros.

You Must Answer Your Phone- Sounds simple, right? On different reviews online, you hear customers say they have left so many messages for real estate agents. The majority of agents do not answer the phone, and most are not busy selling real estate. Answer your phone! Even if you have to tell them you will call them back, they will understand. I have proof from my own experiences that when you respond quickly every time you create a loyal client. Of course, you still have to have Knowledge and Heart. There are messages that you can create on your smart phone that can be polite and all you need to do is click on it if you are on the other line. You are also told not to answer your phone when you are with another client. I do sometimes, especially if I recognize the number. However, what I say goes like the following, "Hi I hope you don't mind if I could please call you back in an hour or so as I am with a very important client just like you and I am going over some details on the home I am showing them right now, I hope you understand? Thanks so much." The client you are with will feel important because they are. Time is such a commodity in today's world; most people understand that.

You will do more business in 2 months than in 2 years if you start asking people about themselves and getting their cards, instead of trying to sell yourself by giving out your card. Once you have their information, you have an opportunity to build and earn a relationship with that person. The other way they could lose your card or worse, throw it out and you will never get that chance.

You Should Have a Laptop, IPad, Tablet or Smart phone- You need to be able to check your emails and have the ability to have access to the MLS.

A lot of success coaches say if you check your emails too often you are not being as productive as you could be.

However, in this business, being the way it is, if it is a 1st email from someone and you wait until the end of day they could possibly email someone who will get back to them sooner. I have someone who I pay to monitor my emails so they can text you or alert you when something that can't wait shows up.

Companies like 123Employee or any VA (virtual assistant company). Make sure they have a good command of the English language. I have made that mistake and learned my lesson. Of course, with your regular clients that refer you, they will wait for you. I have had clients wait for a week for me to get back from a vacation or workshop.

When asked why they didn't want to use one of my agents, they said it was all about the trust level to ensure things were done properly.

Of course, it would be beneficial to have a Coach. According to most studies, those agents that will employ or seek out coaches in their business usually achieve a higher income. Coaches keep you on track and can hold you accountable. Coaches keep your stress level down as they guide you through some tough times in this stressful Industry.

Real Estate is listed as one of the top 3 careers as far as being stressful. Market Pros will help as well with that.

If you don't get a coach, at least go in person to events or conferences where you will rub shoulders with other Market Pros and learn from the speakers and educators there.

Of course, it is great energy when you attend these kind of things; it rejuvenates you and puts you on top of your life again. You will see pictures of me throughout the book with different people who have inspired me, the way I want to inspire you. Unfortunately, a lot of people have been hoaxed, thinking if they just get their Real Estate license, they will make lots of money. The amount of people who quit, the numbers are staggering for the number of people who go to the extent of taking the course, memorizing the books and CDs and passing the test only to find out this is a business that needs you to know so many other things.

An industry constantly changing, throwing new things for you to learn and new places for you to learn about and more important new relationships with new people who might not have been raised like you and don't hold the same morals and beliefs as you. So having your Heart aligned will allow you get along with almost everyone.

Even the couple of people I have fired over the years, I have nicely let them know we were just not aligned. I tried so hard to help and show them what I know best but mean is just mean and no one deserves to be treated like that. This is where I hope you will strive to become a Market Pro in Real Estate by learning from other Market Pros.

My intention with this book is just to give you a glimpse of what is possible and how important it is for likeminded people to come together as a whole and be the difference in someone else's life in a positive manner in the Real Estate Industry.

We have chosen this lifestyle because we love to serve and we love to see results and yes, we also love to make money.

It's ok to do that, we can help a lot of people because of the amount of money that can be made in this business.

I help non-profit charities, painters, landscapers, electricians, plumbers, property management companies, carpenters, handyman, computer geeks, web designers, videographers, the list goes on and on and if we didn't make such good money, how could we help these other businesses with making their living and inspiring them at the same time.

Marketpros.com

WEALTH

Let's define Wealth. I've heard things like a "Wealth of Information", some think "it is just money", while you could be partially right, here is my take on the definition of Wealth.

It has 3 principles or components:

Impact, Inspiration and Income

Impact is 1st because most wealthy people have started on their way to becoming wealthy by having made an impact or made a positive difference in someone else's life by what they have done. In doing that, they felt better inside which leads to Inspiration. Wouldn't you say that a feeling of personal fulfillment and confidence is inspiring? Helping others with their dreams, ZIG ZIGLAR quote says, "You can have everything in life you want, if you will just help enough other people get what they want."

That's where the Income comes in, if you have made an impact and inspired other people in what your expertise is, you will have mastered the 1st 2 components for Wealth.

Would you agree most wealthy people are an expert in something, you too could be wealthy and an expert in Real Estate. By making a huge impact in their lives by finding them a new home or helping them sell their existing home so they can follow through with their end dreams which will inspire them to move forward and guess who makes the money when you do that? YOU.

How many of you know people who have a business but all they are out for is the money. Are they wealthy? Not really, because when you are missing the 1st 2 principals, the 3rd one normally doesn't come unless you win a lottery, and a lot of those people can't hold onto wealth because they do not spend it in a way that makes an impact on others, so they can't get inspired or inspire others.

We have seen this in Real Estate. The ones who when they meet a client for the 1st time, they think how much can I make instead of thinking to themselves how can I help them. I have never done a study on this but I will guess 95% of those who make 6 or 7 figures a year in this business possess the 3 components of Wealth.

Just a part of being a Market Pro with Heart.

YOUR Commissions

You try not to Reduce Your Commissions- I feel that if you truly run your business as a professional and a Market Pro, your clients will see great value in what you offer. Therefore, you will get paid for what you are worth. When you reduce your commissions, it can become an expected thing. However, in certain cases with regular investors, they will remain loyal and they provide your Bread and Butter month after month and for a lot less work if you are doing limited service listings.

When I was going through the lawsuit I won in Supreme Court, I couldn't have made it without my regular investors to help pay for my legal costs.

I have lowered my commission many times just to make the deal work because of other circumstances. Like someone was about to lose their home if it wasn't closed by a certain date and the offers were so close I had to make it work. Other things come up and if you know deep down when you need to be helping someone.

I always like to go by the Golden Rule as far as do unto others as you would have them do unto you.

Would I expect someone to help me if I were in the same situation? A lot of times when someone sells their house with you and then wants to buy one, there is always a potential to give them a contribution towards their closing costs or home warranty.

There are too many situations to name, use your inner voice inside and you determine if you are doing the right thing. Most of the people I have ever helped have referred me at least one if not 5 new clients over the years. The amounts I have ever given up on commissions have come back to me more than five times. Just do the right thing. I was supposed to be at an inspection only because the seller, my client, asked me to be there, part way through I left to

Marketpros.com

tend to another buyer for same client, different property. Consequently, that is when the inspector discovered something that I am paying to have fixed to make up for my seller being angry for me not being there. It's just the right thing. I really don't feel I did anything wrong given the options, but to save time and energy and keep my relationship in tact, I am doing it.

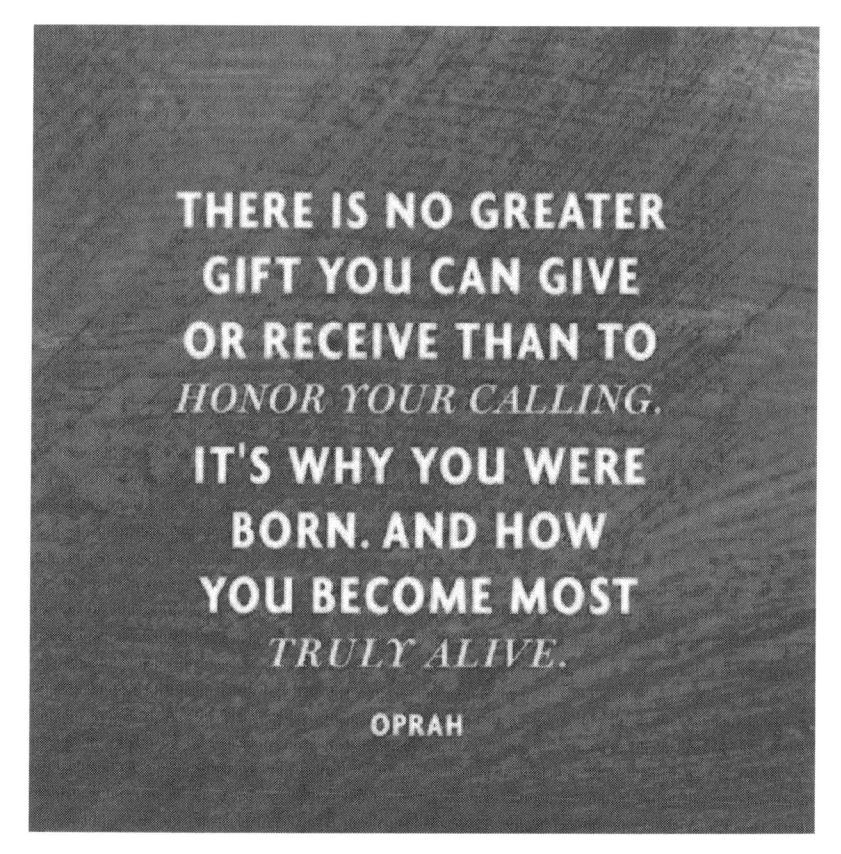

> THERE IS NO GREATER GIFT YOU CAN GIVE OR RECEIVE THAN TO HONOR YOUR CALLING. IT'S WHY YOU WERE BORN. AND HOW YOU BECOME MOST TRULY ALIVE.
>
> OPRAH

BROKER ALIGNMENT

You should Partner with the Right Brokerage for you- If you are working under a franchise or independent, you need to make sure that you are able to GROW your business. Are you able to grow your brand which will grow your business in the long term? Are there too many restrictions with your current brokerage? Will your Broker let you take your contribution to your Buyer or Seller off the top of the commission before the split? There are so many questions to ask... Remember, this is your business! Never take on their email if at all possible as they have the access to that if they own the domain.

I believe Buyers and Sellers don't pick the company, they pick the agent in today's world of technology; they can read reviews online and decide on the actual person. They will soon be able to go online and see if you are a Market Pro to guarantee you have what it takes as far as experience and Heart. I get a lot of my clients who said they picked me after reading reviews and/or after interviewing me over the phone. Align yourself with likeminded people and you will be OK. Don't be afraid to change Brokers if you don't feel like the Broker does not support the Heart Method. I left a large franchise for just that reason. When I confronted the Broker about an agent doing unethical things, she responded in a manner that showed because he was a top producing agent she would just mention something to him. In my brokerage, that person would have been fired. I went back to owning my own Brokerage at that time.

OVERCOMING OBSTACLES

"Challenges are what make Life Interesting and overcoming them is what makes Life Meaningful." - unknown

Always have the end in mind for every transaction. Find solutions always when someone says, "it can't be done", you say then, "How can I make this work". Love this quote.

This world is your best teacher. There is a lesson in everything. There is a lesson in each experience. Learn it and become wise. Every failure is a stepping-stone to success. Every difficulty or disappointment is a trial of your faith. Every unpleasant incident or temptation is a test of your inner strength. Therefore, "nil desperandum. March forward hero!" - Swami Sivananda

We, as Real Estate Professionals and human beings, are very, very good at creating complex relationships where we intertwine, trust, confidence, friendship, and worth into every client we meet, but then when something happens to complicate the transaction or relationship we find, we didn't build in any "safe guards" or "how to's" for problem resolution and find it difficult to resolve conflict or know how to fix it or what to do about it.

We can't really predict the outcome if it is left in someone else's hands, like the lenders, surveyors, the appraisers, underwriters, roofers, plumbers, builders, title companies, attorneys, clients and other agents. Hopefully you have your Inner Circle in place. We know if we hold to the principles, we have established for our life, we will not have to worry about being able to see into the future. Because, when we display trust, we experience trust, when we treat others fairly and honestly, we receive fairness and honesty and when we treat others with respect, we receive respect, in return.

When things go wrong, this is sometimes a challenge to stick to those principles, although I prefer the word distraction when a survey that was promised doesn't show up, or an underwriter who declines the loan at the last minute, or a Buyer who changes their mind. This is truly a distraction. If you were to realize you can't change things that have already occurred, if it is people, place or things. You can make different choices next time. Getting stressed about it can sneak in by way of anxiety, fear and doubt about what someone else is going to say or do and of course what you lose. I like the serenity prayer for situations like that. Can I change anything or is it out of my hands at a certain point.

What I have learned through my training is to acknowledge it, then talk to yourself accordingly "telling yourself this is not the end of the world, I'm still here" let's do the next thing you know what to do that is honest, unselfish and giving instead of burning up energy with anger and resentment.

When this becomes a Habit in your everyday life, it is amazing the stress it eliminates when you can actually look at the situation as part of a lesson. I say every time I am in a situation like this, it somehow makes me feel better. "Even if you lose, just don't lose the lesson"

If you were to treat all your distractions like this, you could have such a wealth of information to not only share with others as I share with you in this book, but also to use as a resource for future relationships.

As human beings, we have a tendency to go back to the way we have always behaved similar to someone who is always attracted to the same type of person even if they know it is not good for them. The three-day boot camp I have planned will be full of problems and more so full of solutions to help guide you through some of the most stressful situations you could imagine in this business. It will be a boot camp like no other as the best solutions require the Market Pros from other professions to help you with yours. Go to Marketpros.com for dates and info.

"We can't solve problems by using the same kind of thinking we used when we created them" - Albert Einstein

RECAP Habits.

Brian Tracy says, "In order to achieve something you have never achieved before you must do something you have never done before."

So what is the magic pill that might prevent us from doing this over again, really, there is no real magic. The magic comes from the foundation we will build our lives on. The gift we get from strong relationships, friendships, that surround us, and people that are in our Inner Circle that are there for us, who will continue to love us and understand us and be there for us and our clients. Imagine if you will, a world without faith, love, hope and joy. There's not much to be happy about, is there? Now imagine a world with all the good things we are gifted in life. Kind of gives you something to look forward to each day, doesn't it? So why do we waste our time on the insignificant things in life that have a negative effect on us and not pour our energy and resources into the things that affect us in a positive manner?

I encourage us to focus on the good things in life. There will always be negative energy around, negative people, however, we have the choice to not allow it to drag us down and affect our lives and our career. I predict you can change your attitude, your path, your life and you can/will make a difference in those around you, because it is a choice you can make each and every day. Choose to

Marketpros.com

be happy, choose to make your life more meaningful, choose to make a difference as a Market Pro in Real Estate.

Unlike most other businesses, the customer is not always right. I say that only because you will encounter non-licensed clients who have been researching online and will insist they know better or just grumpy miserable people. Again, this is where if you are a Market Pro and you truly possess the knowledge of a professional Real Estate Professional you will be able to handle that in a way that does not offend the client. If it does than FIRE THEM (Nicely), when this occurs I usually say, "Please don't take this the wrong way, but this is not a good working relationship and it's probably best you work with another agent." It's like going on a bad date; the chemistry is just not there. One of two things will happen, as I know from experience: 1. They will insist they want to stay with you and will apologize, or 2. They will get an attitude and leave. There are a lot of other potential Buyers and Sellers looking for a Market Pro or Real Estate Professional, so don't sweat it. As long as you have treated that person like they were the most important person on earth. You are wondering why, here it goes. They are the most important as far as they are concerned, as well this is the way human beings, especially Real Estate Professionals should treat all human beings and one another. PERIOD.

There are so many other things involved in being a successful Market Pro that I will have to write it in another book. This is the first of many to come. I will end this in saying that the things you are passionate about are not random, they are your calling. I am passionate about helping the average agent realize the most important parts in becoming a Market Pro with in the Real Estate Industry by making sure the consumer has a heartfelt and positive experience every time. Only then can this occupation regain its integrity and reputation.

GLOSSARY or USEFUL INFORMATION

This is from my Program Wealth Freedom summit for Professional Real Estate Professionals 2014

REFERRALS Means they LIKED WHAT YOU DID AND HOW YOU TREATED THEM

Referral Program Marketing

Strategy: How to Turn Your Customers into Raving Fans That Grow Your Sales

- The HUGE mistake 99% of your competitors are making and how you can profit from it.
- The six reasons why you are not receiving more referrals now and what you can do to increase the number of referrals your clients send you.
- The only way to create a referral marketing system that makes clients proud to refer their friends and family to you.
- How to reward clients and even prospects for referring others to you without spending a fortune.
- How to put your referral marketing campaign on autopilot.

Referrals Are Second Easiest Clients to Close

So, why don't more real estate agents spend time to create a system to consistently produce referrals?

The Harsh Reality…

Like most successful business building strategies, it takes real work and real changes, so many real estate agents avoid it like the plague. 99.9% of agents don't have a single system in place to generate referral business. Most real estate agents are terrible at consistently generating referrals.

Missing the Boat

Easy advertising at little to no additional cost.

Marketpros.com

It's less expensive to generate referrals from existing clients than trying to get new clients. Referrals close at a much higher rate because they've already decided to purchase from you. When you create a referral marketing system, you also create an awesome customer service environment that builds client loyalty.

Why Most Agents Are Not Worthy Of Receiving Referrals

- No real commitment to getting referrals.
- Too much focus on selfish reasons.
- They're not really doing something clients can recommend to others.
- Assuming that a great service alone is enough.
- Afraid of asking for referrals.

The Golden Road…

Level 1: Attracting Suspects
Level 2: Converting Prospects
Level 3: Taking Care of First-Time Clients
Level 4: Inspiring Iron-Clad Loyalty
Level 5: Creating Client Referrals

Generating referrals should be the ultimate goal of all your marketing campaigns!

How to Build Your Referral Generating System
Step #1: Create a List of Ideal Referral Candidates
It's a proven fact that some clients or will send referrals to your business, while others won't. Start by creating a list of profitable clients who are most likely to refer you to others. If you have no way to narrow your list down, then start with a list of 12-24 months of your most recent clients. Try to pinpoint people who have already sent you referrals.

Step #2: Create a Compelling Referral Message
This could be your business U.S.P, but you may also choose to build your referral program around a big benefit. For example, your referral U.S.P could be, guaranteed to sell your house in 120

days or I'll buy it! Focus on what you can do for the client, NOT what the referral means to you.

Step #3: Decide How You Will Reward Your Referrers
In order to create a successful referral reward system, you must know your clients. Some people may get offended at being ethically bribed with gift cards, cash or discounts etc. Luxury items or services = classy rewards (bottle of wine, massage vouchers, etc.) Be sure to follow the guidelines and limitations of your state and governing real estate rules.

Step #4: Create a System to Convert Referrals Into Clients
The value is not in getting the referral, but in converting the referral into a client. Start with one of your existing scripts/presentations and customize it for referral leads. Be sure to include a mention of what the referral qualifies for by being a referral. You should invest training time making sure your scripts/presentations are polished and professional. Take them and make them yours though. You know what feels comfortable to you. Word of Caution: Referrals sometimes have a higher expectation of service

Step #5: Your Referral Follow Up System
Create several marketing pieces based on your core referral marketing message. Make it ALL about the benefit your client gets from referring people to you AND the benefit the referral will receive. Find a creative way to keep your core referral message in front of all your clients.

The Usual Suspects: Use postcards, letters, emails and text messages to follow up with your past clients containing things that will matter to them.

Your referral campaign should ALWAYS be going out to your new clients.

BrakthroughBroker.com is an easy FREE site to go to for real estate newsletters

STORIES I HAVE SENT TO MY DATABASE THAT WERE INSPIRING OR HAD A MORAL TO IT.

Who Stole the Tent

I remember hearing this story about two cowboys out camping one night when the elder of the two awoke in the middle of the night and looked up in amazement at the stars, He woke his young partner and asked him, "When you look up at that bright night sky with all those stars, what does it tell you?" The young partner thought a minute then said, "Well, I'll tell you, in a theological sense it tells me there is a Higher power and we are being watched over; then in an astronomical sense when I see all those stars, it tells me there are other galaxies out there that might sustain life; and in an artistic sense I see a beautiful painting of a bright night sky with a harvest moon in the background." The young cowboy turned to the elder cowboy and asked, "When you're looking up at all those stars, what does it tell you?" To which the elder cowboy replied, "It tells me someone stole our tent."

We all look at things differently, don't we? Some of us look at people or their situation through judgmental eyes, while others look at the same people or situation through loving eyes. Our attitude and gratitude for life is what makes the difference. Some of us have been hurt before, been taken advantage of and we are weary of the kindness and the intention of others. We don't want to experience the pain of a broken heart or the loss of trust again, so we become critical, cynical, and judgmental in our relationships with other people. We stop allowing the closeness of relationships that warm us and we begin to withdraw to the point we feel alone, unwanted and sometimes we think we're a failure or we just accept "it's Ok to be this way". As Real Estate Brokers, we are constantly challenged with looking at life through someone else's eyes whether it is a buyer, seller, or an agent. We constantly have to see their points of view. This is what makes us successful in the Real Estate business.

The biggest challenge does not lie on the shoulders of those agents who do not see through the eyes of potential clients. Since not all agents feel for others like you do and some do not see what others see. It lies on us to be compassionate and teach through example for those who do not truly see as they miss out on what is unseen. There are real opportunities that exist now and the ones that exist in the future. There have been clients that through one agent's eyes that "have wasted my time", while through others we "have guided them" so when they are ready they will come back to us.

The good news is there is hope. We don't have to allow the hurt and pain and missed sales and listings we experienced in the past to take our power or to rule over us in our present. I always say if you lose, just don't lose the lesson. So many times agents carry this stuff around and some even get out of the Real Estate business because it is "just too hard."

Each day when you awake, try to begin your morning being grateful for a new day and a new start. You are the only one who can change and control your outlook and attitude. You are in control of your future and your destiny. Don't allow others to take your power from you or control your dreams and desires.

We need to remember, "Life is 10% what happens to you and 90% how you react to what happens to you." We shouldn't allow the significant few bad things in our life to control the significant many great things we are gifted each day. Take the good things you have and you know about and share them with others.

Family, friends, close relations, clients, people who mimic our walk, all these are the stars in our heaven, tent or no tent.

Take the opportunity to look up, give thanks for your gifts and talents, and look at your future through loving eyes. This is your chance to have a whole new world opened to you that will enlarge your vision and imagination.

I encourage us today to search for and find the joy and happiness life and this career has to offer us. Look within, move the "stuff" out of the way that is blocking your inner most dreams and desires. Take the good stuff off the shelf. Dust them off. Shine them up and display them for the world to see.

Marketpros.com

You have the power within to be become more than you thought you could become, do more than you ever thought possible and be the person you always wanted to become.

ANOTHER STORY TO USE FOR INSPIRATION, TO SHARE WITH YOUR DATABASE

The Lady with the Dead Duck

A lady takes her lifeless duck into the vet for him to examine. The Vet lays the duck on the table, puts his stethoscope on the ducks body, looks at the woman and says, "I am sorry your duck is dead." The woman screams, "How can you say that without running tests on it?" The Vet rolls his eyes, leaves the room and returns with a Labrador retriever. The dog sniffs the duck from head to toe then looks at the Vet and shakes his head. Then the Vet leaves the room and comes back with a Cat. The cat looks the duck up and down then looks at the Vet and shakes his head. The Vet says, "It's confirmed the duck is dead." The woman said, "Well okay, how much do I owe you?" he Vet says, "$150 dollars." The woman angrily replied, "How can you charge $150 dollars to tell me my duck is dead." The Vet replied, "It's normally $20 dollars, but with the Lab report and the Cat scan that brings the total to $150 dollars."

When we don't address issues and life's challenges, allowing them to accumulate they become larger than expected and more difficult to manage. In my life, I have let things I had no control over, something insignificant, steal my joy. I worried over it, lost sleep because of it, allowed it to change my attitude, affect my well-being until it had grown into something unrecognizable, I was carrying it around with me all day like my heavy purse over my shoulder.

However, when I actually took the time to resolve it, the issue was, well, a non-issue. I had manifested it in my mind into something that I thought was a real problem or obstacle keeping me from my goal.

That's what happens when we worry. Worrying about an issue and not stepping up to resolve it takes our joy and happiness. We get bogged down, change into someone no one recognizes and honestly, maybe someone who others choose to not associate with because of our attitude. We feel alone as if no other person has ever experienced the issue and find ourselves totally withdrawn from the world. We shouldn't allow this to happen.

We should address every issue as it comes along. It's like the old adage, "How do you eat an elephant? One bite at a time." It may take you longer than you want it to take, and you may get tired of eating only elephant for dinner, but if you are diligent, over time, only the skeleton will remain.

Life's too short to allow issues to build and worry over them. It is best to address them as they come along as difficult as it seems at times, look at the alternative. Do you want to use up all your energy on something that gets you nowhere and most likely the other people have no idea nor care what you are going through. Ok so how do I handle this? If the issue is with another person and its conflict you fear, enlist a friend to help with the resolution. It may be a simple misunderstanding between you and the other person and it helps to have a mediator. If it's a money issue, take the time to review your finances. You may be spending more on things you want than on the things you need. If it's your job or career that is the issue, take the time to write the things you like about your job and the things you don't like. More than likely, you will find the like column longer and that the issue may be your attitude. Make the choice to change either one depending how it turns out.

No one is immune to problems. They are part of everyday life. Every problem is an opportunity to learn something new. Each learning experience helps you to stretch and grow into the person you are destined to become. At any given time most people are either in the middle of a crisis, have just come out of a crisis, or are heading into a crisis. Right?

Each time we have an obstacle in our path, we can, either turn around and avoid it, or we can find a way under, over, around, or through. We can't allow a little, bitty, insignificant issue steal our joy and happiness, can we? No, we can't, and no we won't. So next time you face an issue, face it with confidence, resolve it, then

Marketpros.com

evaluate what you learned from it to prevent the same from happening in the future.

I encourage us today to look ahead and anticipate life's issues with knowing you can and will resolve them before they arrive or at least shorten the experience. Reach out to others and get their advice. You'd be surprised how many others, especially successful individuals, have experienced similar issues and they are still here and doing fine. Face them with confidence and maintain a teachable spirit so you can learn from the experience and it will make a difference in your life and the lives of those around you.

A Thanksgiving Message Email I sent to my clients (tweak for your clients)

At this time of Thanksgiving as I pause to count my blessings (which for those that know me well, the pause doesn't happen too often), I am trying to learn how to meditate. LOL. I am reminded of the following and hope you don't mind me sharing these.

1. The fact that our life is a gift.

2. Failure is an Event not a person, you can't always keep what you have but you can keep who you are.

3. Difference between and a Dream and a Goal...A Dream reaches inside you and stays there, a goal is a place or thing you want to get to and is only temporary.

4. It's not just important to deliver the message, but be the message, even if it takes working on the messenger.

5. Getting from Desperation to Inspiration when you are at the end of your rope, tie a knot.

6. Long lasting Happiness is not a place when you get there or a material thing you get, it's what you are and who you become while

getting to that place or the feeling while becoming Victorious in getting the things you want.

7. Forgiveness is not forgetting, Forgiveness is remembering without Anger.

8. People form Habits, Habits create Futures; Habits are too light to be felt until they are too heavy to be broken.

9. Be thankful for what you have; you'll end up having more. If you concentrate on what you don't have, you will never, ever have enough. (Research shows that people are happier if they are grateful for the positive things in their lives, rather than worrying about what might be missing)

If you are receiving this email, then you have had a positive impact or made a difference of some kind in my life from just knowing you.

To my Family, I appreciate the love and lessons we have shared together.

To my clients or those who I have met through Real Estate, I appreciate your friendship and confidence you have shown in me and the lessons I have learned from you as well.

My friends, I am thankful for you being there when we have laughed and cried together or just been there to give me hope and guidance and support.

To my business partners and associates I have worked with, thanks for the mutual respect and friendship and for just being there.

For all of these things and so much more, I am very thankful. My best wishes for a Happy Thanksgiving!

Marketpros.com

SCRIPTS I HAVE USED THAT WORKED FOR ME (make them your own)

COLD LEAD Subject Line: Responding to your email about _____ from (your name)

#1 Hi _____

I just received your email and wanted to get back to you as soon as possible and to reach out to you to let you know that I did get the message. I have considerable knowledge in this area and would love to be able to help you, unless of course you already have a working relationship with a Real Estate Professional. I don't like stepping on someone else's toes, if you know what I mean.

If not, I am very willing to give you 110% of my time and knowledge as a Professional Market Pro Real Estate Professional here in this area.   I am available pretty well most of the time so feel free to contact me anytime with any additional questions or requests you might have.

I look forward to hearing from you soon, hope this information helps as a start. I appreciate the opportunity to help you.

#2 Hi _____

I received your email request from _either Zillow or Real Estate Professional.com or your website_____ and here is what I know about this property,

(GIVE DETAILS OFF MLS) I will send you a full report here in a few minutes with photos.

If you want to send me your criteria," your absolute have to have "and your "for sure I don't want" or "it would be nice to have" I can look for deals and when they come up you will be first to know, as you can see real estate sales have picked up in this area and the good ones go very quickly. I look forward to helping you. Feel free to call me anytime, in this business we need to have a communication level so you get exactly what you are looking for at the best price. I appreciate the opportunity to help you.

Thanks and hope to talk soon

#3 Hi,

I just needed to get back to you with regard to your request. I am not sure what your name is as it didn't come through on the email you sent to me. It's kind of like a blind date. LOL

Any way here is the info you requested, If you haven't already formed a relationship with a Real Estate Professional from this area here in _____ then I would love to be your "GoTo" Market Pro or Real Estate Expert that you depend on for any answers, for emails about stats and the area or especially keep you abreast of when something comes on the market that matches what you are looking for.

Please feel free to reach out and call me anytime, I look forward to speaking to you in person and appreciate the opportunity to help you.

 (If you go to www.pipl.com you can sometimes get their personal information just from an email address)

Join MarketPros for a whole list of websites and apps that will help you in your real estate business. Go to MarketPros.com

Marketpros.com

INTERVIEWS FROM MY SPEAKING EVENT Wealth Freedom Summit for Professional Real Estate Professionals IN TAMPA OCTOBER 2014

Russ Whitney, Real Estate Guru, Developer, Author, Thought Leader

Kerry: What is it that was important to you when you were in that industry? What were you looking for in a Real Estate Professional? What was one of the most important things to you in a Real Estate Professional that you were using or utilizing?

Russ: Can I be honest?

Kerry: Yes, absolutely.

Russ: Oh, so I do that. I tell you, I'm going to give you a quick tour of my office because that's where you are now. But I don't know if you could see it or not. So I'm going to go right around that circle. I have to make you a bit dizzy.

You can see all the books. You can see all the-- Here we go. And so now you got a whirlwind view of my office. This is about 1,000 square feet and the building is about 12,000. This is where I do all my writing and so forth from.

They say, by the way, Kerry, you were mentioning that real estate isn't my mainstay, although just up maintaining. And right now I'm building a 480-unit project in Costa Rica which is about 2/3 single-family homes and 1/3 condos. You'll love this probably.

I'm in Florida by the way. I'm down in Southwest Florida in the Fort Myers, Cape Coral, Sanibel Island area, and from 2000 to 2006 or 2007, just before the bust, my construction company built about 7,000 homes. We were the third largest builder here. We did work a lot with Real Estate Professionals.

You say, "what am I looking for in a Real Estate Professional?" It depends on what the project is. For example, I categorize Real Estate Professionals in a couple of different categories. One is what we would call a 'scrap Real Estate Professional' and the other is what we would call a 'crème of the crop Real Estate Professional.'

The crème of the crop Real Estate Professional is generally, because of the new construction homes, we're generally just getting the Real Estate Professional that wants to show the three-bedroom, two-bath home in the nice school district or what have you. A lot of those were investor homes as well so we had pre-sold most of that to construction.

So I see Real Estate Professionals in two categories, well, maybe three. I see them in a category of the ones that work for the bigger franchises, maybe the Century 21s, etcetera. Those are good for the new construction business.

But in the investment business which is where I was for the first 30 years, 25, 30 years in my career, I own hundreds and hundreds and hundreds of apartment units both up in New York where I started and down here in Florida. But for those units, I would use what we call a scrap Real Estate Professional. And the scrap Real Estate Professional is the one who works the low and moderate income areas and generally the multi-unit residential.

This is the Real Estate Professional that I would look for that's either a brand new Real Estate Professional that I can train so I don't have to unteach them bad habits. And the scrap Real

Estate Professional is generally the one I would look for in a low-moderate income neighborhood because my niche was providing decent, safe, and affordable housing for low and moderate-income people. Generally, those were anywhere from a duplex on up to 100-unit building.

So I'm looking for that Real Estate Professional that's working that area that has some investment expertise. My general call would be, "Hi. This is Russ Whitney. I buy income-producing properties. I'm looking for properties from a duplex on up to 50-unit building. We're looking primarily for cosmetically-distressed properties and we do all of our own work. I'm looking primarily for seller financing. Do you have any properties that fit those parameters?"

Normally, what I would get when I would start prospecting is whoever is on floor duty and when you get the floor duty person, you may or may not get an experienced Real Estate Professional. And so you generally get a couple of different responses. When I gave that little presentation there of a duplex on up to 50 units, cosmetically-distressed, looking for seller financing, the first response I would get would be this. Yes, like no response.

The second response to that would be, "Well, you know, I have to research that so let me get back to you and I'll send you some listings." Usually, what you get there is them trying to sell their own listings rather than find the right properties suited for what I'm asking for. And I can always tell that.

And if I get the first like that, I would then ask, "Is there somebody in your office that specializes in multi-unit residential or commercial properties and who would be the top producer?" If I didn't

	get a good answer there then I'd ask for the broker and I'd go right to the broker. Talking to the broker, I would get a sense of whether they even handle anything like that. So that's kind of long-winded answer but did that help?
Kerry:	Yes. Did that help everybody a little bit?
Speaker 16:	Yes.
Kerry:	Okay, good. Another question that you might have for somebody who's been really, really successful in dealing with real estate? I mean, if you were a Real Estate Professional and you were after somebody who was – how much commissions would - like did you stick with one Real Estate Professional your entire time when you were investing? Did you have one main Real Estate Professional that you got along with? He did well or she did well for you?
Russ:	No. Well, you know what? Well, yes and no. When I first started like at 20 years old which would be about seven years ago…
Kerry:	Right. Me, too. Starting out, that is.
Russ:	You find that very funny, huh? Anyway, I got my own real estate license initially when I was about 23 years old and because I didn't have a lot of money that allowed me to go out and prospect income-producing properties, and if I was buying, I would also get to sell in commission so it would help me reduce the down payment. But as I started to grow, other brokers or other Real Estate Professionals would be gun-shy about working with me because they think they do all the work and then I might out them from the commission. So what I do is I gave up my real estate license at that point.

Marketpros.com

So I would work with numerous Real Estate Professionals because of the volume that I was doing. And there were always saying, this same old rule, the 80/20 rule, 20% do 80% of the volume. But really I look more for the 2% person, one who is the two percenter. And generally, that would be somebody that had income-producing property experience.

So I would always look for a Real Estate Professional that also was an owner of income-producing properties especially in that low and moderate income category because when you're first getting started, that's where the cash flow is. So if you want to build a real estate business, you hear about short sales and the wholesaling and all this gimmick you think. Those are really more entrance and exit strategies.

If you want to build a real estate business really, you would go to the Donald Trumps, the Russ Whitneys, the Sam Zells, the Conrad Hiltons, and the bigger ones who did it in a bigger fashion. We all did it the same way. Every one of us started in low and moderate income property. As we got cash to roll, we were able to put more equity into the more upper scale properties. But in those upscale properties, you can get better appreciation but not as much cash flow.

Speaker 18: Yes.

Russ: When I'm looking for low and moderate income properties and multi-unit residential, commercial is a little different, warehouse is a little different, but in a multi-unit residential, that was the approach I would take; to find somebody that was green and then train them on how to prospect. If I don't think they weren't experienced enough, I would go up to the broker

101

to find out who was the most experienced person in the office for multi-unit residential.

And for cosmetic-distressed, because you know what, some Real Estate Professionals, most especially the new ones, their modus operandi is finding a three bedroom, two bath home with green carpets and nice closets in a school district. That would not be the better person that I'd be looking for. I'd be looking for somebody that really went to hammer out buying.

Kerry: Got it. Okay. Alright. Thank you. One last question. Did you ever have a Real Estate Professional that you can remember their name and the relationship you had with them back when you were buying and selling homes? Was there one Real Estate Professional that ever stood out that you can remember right now?

Russ: There are numbers of them. The first one I ever worked with when I was 20 years old, I haven't seen him in probably 30 years, but his name is Gary Sanders. And I remember calling around when I had first bought my first get-rich book in real estate. It was a book called "How To Wake Up The Financial Genius Inside You."

And I was 20 years old, haven't graduated high school, I was working in a slaughterhouse for $6.50 an hour. I was married and had a child on the way so I wasn't a free-willing bachelor at 20 years old. And I got this voice in my head that told me I could do something better with my life. And I didn't even know what that meant back then.

My newest book is called the "Inner Voice." I wouldn't have called it that back then. Just for you guys' knowledge there, aside from real estate investor, I've written 30 books on real estate investing. Three of them are New York Times bestsellers.

"Building Wealth" is still on bookstore shelves today. The other iscalled "Millionaire Real Estate Mentor." And the other is called "The Millionaire Real Estate Mindset." I don't really make my living on the selling of those books. They're relatively low-priced. You could buy them at Amazon or anywhere.

But I would say "Building Wealth" would categorize that first direction I told you about which is buying low and moderate income residential units. And that is until you obtain financial independence. And literally my goal is to become a millionaire.

When I read this book, I was 20 years old. This book, first of all, had two concepts. Little one concept taught, if you go to an area of town and look for properties there in run-down and beat-up shape, paint them, clean them, jazz them up, you could force the value up, kind of with the cosmetic improvements. So you don't hang around and hope the market goes up to make you money in real estate. That's the amateur way to do it. Here, we go and win and we force the value up with improvements.

It also had a mathematical formula, that said, you could figure out whether or not you can make the money on real estate or in real estate investing before you eve buy the property so you reduce your risk. That formula, and it's as simple as a formula is, simply add up the projected rents.

So you have the duplex each side, rent is for 1,000 bucks, you got 2,000 coming in. Deduct your projected expenses, tax, insurance, water, sewer, maintenance, vacancy, and if there's

103

money left over, that's positive cash flow. Or you take that positive cash flow, divide it into the down payment and that gives you a rate of return. So I always look for at least the 20% cash on cash return.

But more importantly, this book said that I could be a millionaire and I was just ignorant enough at 20 years old, without any worldliness to believe it. What I had latched onto is that "millionaire." Three weeks after I bought this book, I used the technique out of the book called the seller subordination technique and I made $11,000 on a piece of property in three weeks to a month.

And I took all of the money that I made and I invested into two more run-down, beat-up properties like duplex, triplex type of properties and I ran out of the money to fix them up because I was so inexperienced. So I had to start hunting around for a home improvement loan and I got turned down, turned down, turned down not because I had bad credit but I had no credit. I was only 21 years old.

And finally, I got this one Real Estate Professional or not a Real Estate Professional but a banker. He said, "You don't qualify for home improvement loan but we can probably get you an FHA Title I loan. In my ignorance, of course, I said, "Yes, that's exactly what I was thinking." But I didn't know what he was talking about.

But anyway, with the FHA Title I loan, it's a government-insured loan, which the government came up with this idea to get banks to stop redline. So redlining, banks in a lot of run-down areas don't want to lend the money. So they're discriminating really in the low-income and the ethnic area.

Back then, you could borrow up to $17,500 and the government would insure the loan 90%. So if I go to the bank and I borrow $17,000, if I default, the government pays the bank back 90% of that loan. So it was a very low-risk loan for the bank and the credit requirements weigh less. So what I did is I found out anywhere in the United States, if you own the property, you could be your own contractor and you don't have to have a license. So I could be the general and hire the plumber and so forth.

So what I did was that I just used my common sense and I started my own contracting company. My wife's name is Ingrid. My name is Russ so the company was R & I Enterprises. "No job too big or too small, R & I does it all."

I got some contractor's estimate for the $6,000 to $7,000 to fix the property up. I rewrote my contractor's estimate for the $17,000. So I borrowed the $17,000, the cash flow, from the properties to cover it. Now, that gave me another $8,000 for down payment on two more pieces of property.

I just kept that going for about two years. At 23, I was able to quit my job. I had achieved financial independence. I wasn't rich but I had enough money coming in off the rentals to pay my mortgage payment, car payment, put the food on the table. And I have a little luxury money left over without having to go to a full time job.

And I continued to feed my mind. I bought every book I could get my hands on investing in real estate or marketing and business. Over the next four years, by the time I hit 27 years old, I hit a net worth of a million dollars. And that is when I wrote my first book on how I did it. That was in 1984.

Kerry: That's great. That's great.

Russ: So I would suggest, there's a suggestion to you that if you're really full time, serious Real Estate Professional, the no-money down, the low and moderate income stuff, this is a great marketplace that most Real Estate Professionals overlook because they don't know about it.

But right now, there's such a proliferation on the internet of these real estate investment training, books and home study courses that I think there's a great market, a customer market for you in that field.

It would be certainly worth looking into it. If I were you I would.

Kerry: Russ has another business that I really wanted him to share with you as well. If you don't mind talking about the "Inner Voice," how you started that and why you started it and all that, I think they'd be interested in.

Russ: Sure. Be happy to. After I wrote my book, my book was published by 1984 company called the publishing company called the "National Institute of Financial Planning". They hosted big real estate conferences all over the country.

The book, you got to remember, I'm 27 years old, I only have seven years of experience. I write this book. I think it was just done in such a layman's way with people going to understand it. I made it simple. They loved it.

They sent it and they published the book but I have to agree to go to speak at their conferences to promote the book. I would be brought to 6,000-, 2,000-person conferences and speak on what I did, I really just showed pictures of

Marketpros.com

properties, how I pulled the money out, and how I leveraged the properties for loan.

I thought everybody knew about this because I didn't graduate at high school. Most of the people come here at summer was college-educated. All I did was buy some rundown beat up properties and get them to cash flow. I figured everybody knew that.

While I did these seminars I would be mobbed; 90% of the crowd mobbed me wanting more information on this. The things that I share and teach, you don't learn in grade school, high school or college.

Anyway, I ended up building a financial training company. I was up and down, up and down. I still had hundreds of apartment units. But I really like sharing the strategies that I had learned to get the financial independence and millionaire with people. People really welcomed it.

It was up and down, up and down, so I had to learn a whole new business. The seminar in Financial Education business is a different animal from investing in real estate.

In 1996 I developed what we call continuity training programs. They were 18-month to three-year continuity training programs. From 2000 to 2006, I had over 60,000 people a month attending our live events in seven countries. We were putting on six to seven live events a week, and the company went from-- 1996, we did $5 million in revenue. The next year is $13 million, and $26 million, $60 million, $90 million, and all the way up in 2005, we were doing over a quarter of a billion dollars a year in sales.

107

I took that company public. We went from 14 cents to $14. I had 5.5 million shares, $14 unencumbered, you do the math. A big number there $70 to $80 million.

Also in 2000, it became a good outlet for us because the market was so good. We started building new construction homes for investors. As I told you, from 2000 to 2006 we've built over 7,000 homes. That business did another 750 million in revenue.

But that's all the good news, by the way. In 2006 we came under investigation by the Securities and Exchange Commission and the Department of Justice which is the IRS of steroids. You don't necessarily have done anything wrong. I'm under investigation.

But they were making some allegations that are really heinous. They wanted me to enter into a voluntary compliance or settlement with them. I refused to do it because it just wasn't so.

I had 2,000 employees who are high-level executives. They all came out of Fortune 500 companies where they'd run $500 million to billion dollar business units. We had 20 lawyers on staff. It's not like you're walking to a department and wink, wink, nod, nod and say, "Let's cheat people, today." It doesn't work that way.

Over the next four years I spent $22 million on legal fees battling this. At the end of those four years there was no finding of any wrong-doing whatsoever, no sanction, no fine, nothing. They both closed their cases, walked away.

But during that time period because of the bad press, a thousand people lost their jobs in our company. The stock went from $14 to 14 cents. I

Marketpros.com

lost. That's in 2006, I was heavily invested in real estate.

I lost over 80% of my net worth which was about in excess of a $100 million at that time. You know what? After 30 years of working my butt off doing the right thing, I just threw my hands up and said, "You know what, God, what is the point? What am I here for?"

I have billions of dollars on a private jet, Rolls Royce, Ferrari, based the family. Also, the life crashing came. I have lots of failures along the way. You're hearing about my successes. But for every success there's probably four failures to get to that success.

What I did? As I walked away from that company, I was ousted from it. I put management into my other businesses. Although I wasn't broke, I was humiliated in front of my peers, in the industry, and my family.

I'd say, you can almost call it a nervous breakdown. I just can't at this point. I was over 50 years old, starting to experience mortality, feeling like I was running on a hamster wheel my whole life--if you think about it, most of us do-- go to work, get a job, find a spouse, get a car, build a business, have some crisis along the way, whatever it is. Every once in a while we have a good family or vacation day where you say "life is good".

Then we're back on the hamster wheel again. I don't care if you make $50,000 or $5 million. It's the same hamster wheel. Then, 60 years later we die.

I was thinking to myself, if that's all the risk to this life, and there is a God, or an organization to this universe, it would have to be a really mean one if that was what this whole life was about.

I have two questions. What's the purpose of life? What's the point? And, who's right? Are the Christians right? Are the Jewish people right? Are the Muslims right? Are the Hindus right? Is Kerry Jackson right? Phil Donahue, Oprah Winfrey, who's right?

I went on a 20 country tour over the last five years, now it's in the six years now. This is where I devoted my life to. I walked away from all the mundane business.

I visited Abu Dhabi, Dubai, Israel, Haiti, Columbia, Spain, Europe, and South America. I get to work to some of the top religious spiritual and business leaders worldwide because of the books and the size of the business that gives me access whether that's fair or not I don't know but it's just is.

I found some amazing answers. They changed my life. My life is completely different now than it was six years ago and prior. I never said I have to write a book either. I really said I have to save my own life and figure it out.

It ended up two years ago in an offer from one of the largest spiritual publicists in the world which is Hay House. They do.

I had no credibility in that arena at all but they saw my writings. We got to talk and they offered me one of the largest advances I've ever seen for a book and told me they would help me make this a book.

Here's the Club. The book is called, "The Inner Voice, Unlock Your Purpose and Passion".

Marketpros.com

Although it's not a religious book, it doesn't conflict with any religion. It only enhances.

Although it's not a book about success or making money, it's everything about success and making money.

The short overview is that if you go to Amazon, you look on Amazon.com for Inner Voice. You'll see it's got five star reviews from all over the world. Better reviews in any book I've ever written.

It's really touching a nerve worldwide in people because there's a lot of people with that same question who've gone through a lot of turmoil over the last five, six or ten years, whatever it is.

People who've lost their homes, the economy is There's a lot of people right now that are in anxiety, frustration, fear, doubt. They're carrying a lot of guilt shame and resentment from the past which I had done so.

Anyway, in this book I talk in two voices. I talk in the voice of a warrior and I talked in a voice of a statesperson. The warrior I categorized as age 20 to 40. From age 20 to 40 we operate almost solely on human training.

What Mom, Dad, brother, sister, preacher, teacher put in our brain. That usually centers around selfishness, self-centeredness, arrogance, finger-point, judging, blaming, criticizing, sarcasm, self-pity, victim, to name a few.

We chase a lot of rabbits that we don't catch during those years because we're running totally on self-will. I was the foster boy for that. I can simply attest to that.

Here's what I found on my travels. What I found is I travelled country to country to country working in all the different religious and spiritual beliefs. There's a lot of commonalities at the top.

What happens at around 40 is where we enter the statesperson era of life. Some get it at 35 to 37. But it usually comes as a result of a life crushing.

Either life crushes us health, tragedy of some sort. We get crushed in a relationship with a significant other, child, whatever. The most common is we crush ourselves in self-sabotage.

This is where we realized we've been running on this hamster wheel when I starting to experience mortality at 40, we're realizing this journey is going to end. Did I sing the song I was supposed to sing? Am I living in my purpose? Am I stepping up to the purpose that God put me on this planet to step up to?

Most people have no idea how to get to that place and I didn't either until I went on to this journey. As you read the book you'll feel like you are in this journey with me. I get people call me all the time talking about, Herman, or Jose, or some of the characters in the book that are really real people They're not just characters.

If you can't take five years off and go on to this journey, you'll feel you're going along with me. While I'm probably winning your appetite with a lot of this stuff, I just want to read you this.

Instead of going to Amazon because you're at Kerry's event and she's one of our coaching clients, we agree with her that we do something very special for you.

	What I'd like to do is give you the book for free. How many of you in the room would like to get it for free?
Kerry:	Everybody.
Russ:	That's not a hard close, is it? Not like selling a house at all.
	Here's what you need to do. You'll go to this web address. wilter.innervoicewag.com.
	You don't have to put in the www, don't do that. Just go to wilter.innervoicewag.com. That will take you to a website where you can hold your information
	I'm not going to send you a digital copy. I'm going to send you a natural hard cover collector's edition. All you have to do is pay the shipping and handling which is $6.97 and we'll ship you the book free.
	When you go in to Amazon you'll see it's at 20 bucks or more. You're getting a real value.
	But here's what else I'm going to do. I'm going to send you eight free videos. We sell them for $500. I'm going to send them to you for free. They're 35 to 50 minutes long. They take the Inner Voice message a thousand feet deeper.
	We have big review. You'll be very wowed with the content. The other thing we're going to do is we're going to give you two assessment calls. That means we're going to allow you to talk to one of our Inner Voice certified coaches, probably we'll get you one that's both certified Inner Voice and a real estate. Those are generally valued to $500. We're really going to give you $1788 worth of what we call swag bonuses for

free. Just pay for the shipping and handling of the book.

Is that a fair deal?

Kerry: That's fabulous. Thank you.

As a matter of fact, Russ, I talked to his office. We actually set up a domain name, it's called turningyourlifearound.com if that's easier to remember. If you forget that, go to turningyourlifearound.com and they'll take you to exactly the same thing as a Real Estate Professionalswag/

Like me, I'm over 55, I'm starting a little funny on the slash. Is it forward, backward, I don't know.

Russ: 55, you're just a kid.

Kerry: I know. Thank you. Everyone's thanking you for that.

Russ: Once we go to this life crushing we start to experience this mortality and we start to question. Had our life been meaningful? If not, what's the point of it all?

I found some amazing answers there. Generally, what we find when we hit the stage arena we get crashed and humbled, we start to figure out or find this message. That is the power of humility, the power of tolerance, the power of patience, the power of kindness, the power of letting go of resentments, and the power of forgiveness.

At the pathway to purpose, most people like me probably I hear all those sound advice, those wonderful words, humility, tolerance, patience, kindness, letting go of resentments, forgiveness. Most people do not know how to do it.

We can define those things but how do you actually do those things and turn them into a power to your business? Does that make sense there?

I looked at those things as weaknesses. Today I understand they're extreme powers. In this book, it is not a book either. There's a tool or action plan for it. It starts with understanding what the game of life is about.

We understand soccer and baseball. We run on our hamster wheel. We get our test on. But how many have ever stopped to get a chance to step off that hamster we all say, "You know what? What is the whole point here? What's the game of life about?"

Here's what the game of life about. The game of life is a search for the truth, a daily search for the truth with you and the God of your understanding. The time clock for the game of life contrary to popular belief is not 80 or 85 years. It is today.

At all levels of religion and spirituality that I have worked with, at all of with this commonality, and that is that God did not build us with enough energy for tomorrow, next week, or next year.

We've only been built for energy for today. When we get it into tomorrow, or next week, or next year here's what we get. We get anxiety, frustration, fear, doubt, guilt, and shame.

The reason is we start playing the "what if" game. What if this, what if that, what if this, what if that? We create this whole bunch of anxiety where 98% never even comes God gives us a lot of examples in nature.

For example, have you ever seen two birds on an electric wire having nervous breakdown? Because they live in today. It's a good example. They don't even know where the next meal is coming from.

But most of us end up living in tomorrow. That's where the blocks come. If you're not yet selling in your real estate business, if you're not selling and you're feeding your mind, and you think you're doing all the right things, most people, when I've had 6 million people go through my training events over the last 20 or six million, most of them do not fail because they don't understand the marketing techniques or the sales techniques.

They fail because life gets in the way. House bill issues, wife issues, car issues, financial issues, crisis issues that come.

In the game of life, we start at tomorrow. We bring in today because we don't have enough energy for tomorrow or next week or next year. We certainly were not built with energy for yesterday.

When we go to yesterday, generally we go there for guilt, shame and resentment which is also a total waste of time.

The object is to try to keep it in a moment. In the "Inner Voice" book we give you a ton of exercises that are real life experiences. Not a lot of advice or opinions, this book is written with experience, strength, and hope.

That is, did I have an experience like yours or many like yours along the way? If so what did I learn along this journey that a 50 years old has taught me how to handle completely different and why is my life better because of that.

Marketpros.com

I thank God this. Although you can go to all the training events in the world, the "Inner Voice" piece is the missing piece of the puzzle for most people.

Now, let's go to the scoreboard. What is the scoreboard of life? How do we know whether we're winning or losing? My score board used to bigger car, bigger jet, new Rolls Royce, next business deal, next merger, next acquisition, That's out of balance.

The universe is made of energy and energy has to balance. If we're out of balance for too long, the energy will deal a crisis. I'll get to that in a minute. But in the game of life, search for the truth, a daily search for the truth with you and the God you understand how do you do with that? You do that with a process we call two-way conscious contact which is in this book.

The score board is for me today, my score board is at the end of the day, what is my ratio of being happy, joyful, and spiritually free with the absence of anger, anxiety, frustration, fear, doubt, guilt, shame.

The work, the buy product, and the money, that will all come. But when we're living in tomorrow or yesterday we totally back ourselves from the gift that the universe wants to give us.

I'll give you an example. Most people think that the universe or that God looks like Moses. He floats around the sky and takes score.

I thought that for years. Kerry, that means you are impatient today. You worked nice to the lady at the 7/11 and you drove too fast. That's going to be two ingrown toe nails, one flat tire, and a bad real estate year.

Obviously we know that's not the way it works but that's how most people thought process go. God created what He called immutable laws of universe. I like to look at this Inner Voice book as a playbook for life because life really...is your choice.

INTERVIEW OCT 2014 (on Youtube)

ROBERT DRAKE Broker Developer, Trusted Real Estate Advisor to Multimillionaire Clients

    The last part of the day, today. I've saved a very special person, that has come to us via New York. But he is actually living in Cape Coral, Florida right now. And this is a very special person that I've met as a client and it's been really, really interesting. Him, how he's come in to my world as far as real estate. And I was wanting him to, may be explain exactly how we met. As I said, because Robert... This is Robert Drake; he has a background in Hedge Funds which I'm going to get him to explain. You found properties for Hedge Fund Investment Groups?

Robert Drake: Yes, we packaged... We used Hedge Funds money, bought groups then packaged them up and then resold them off again.

Kerry Jackson: Right.

Robert Drake: In some neat stuff and neat ways.

Kerry Jackson: And that was in the real estate boom, when that was going on.

Robert Drake: No, At the end of the boom because when all the foreclosures were there.

Marketpros.com

Kerry Jackson:	When all the foreclosures were there? So he was in a very, very interesting story. But I think even more interesting story as it relates to getting to the heart of the matter, which is my entire three days is about how important it is to have those things, those five behaviors aligned, right? So I want Robert to tell you the story of exactly how we met. And how we ended up doing business together and how I ended up being able to have the opportunity to make substantial income or will be making substantial income by working with him and how it all kind of evolved. Would everyone like to hear that?
Audience:	Absolutely.
Kerry Jackson:	Okay, Robert, go ahead.
Robert Drake:	I'll just give you a little background, you know, will shortly introduce why I came down here from New York, work with the Hedge Funds, working with some real big players in the market. As the market change, in that time I stumbled across a place called, "Lehigh Acres." After doing some research, stumble on, found Cape Coral and found this boom, which turned out to be the third of the largest boom in bus towns. I said, "I'm going there." Do I have any connections down here? No. Had I ever been? No. Had I ever put my foot in the Gulf of Mexico? No. Okay? But I could see the opportunity down here. So, I had no investor base. No, clients base. No, pure anything, I had a lot of investors from, some from New York, a lot from California, you know, various places. We were doing cash flow stuff, I got down to Florida, I studied this land market. I watched what it happened, I studied it graphically. I graphed everything back myself, I run all my numbers

119

from 1999 forward and saw this. And I gain the knowledge of the market.

Then I got with the brokerage, the broker handed me a client. "Here's this guy. He's an investor buying properties and selling them overseas throughout those real investors. Make it work." Sold him couple lots, first week or two. Ended up selling, probably last year, two hundred fifty lots. I don't even know the numbers with this guy. But from there, everything started to evolve. I started to become in less than a year, "The land guy" in Cape Coral. But I talked to people... Also and people are coming to me, Real Estate Professionals are coming to me. I've got this guy; he wants to buy lots. So we're putting together lots of deals. People are bringing me investors too, okay?

Kerry Jackson: So do you think Robert, that may be your habits have something to do with that?

Robert Drake: Absolutely.

Kerry Jackson: And your ethics. You think so?

Robert Drake: And the key to that is, when a Real Estate Professional would bring somebody. I told them straight up front, "I'm going to take care of you." And a lot of times, I didn't know how yet. But they trusted me and especially after a couple of deals with me, that trust was Real Estate Professionals would send me their own people, you know. He's in town, can you drive him around and show him?" "Yes. Absolutely." Okay. And then, we figure out how much we make and then we'll deal it. We'll split it up and some way that's fair for both of us. Because you know what? I want him to tell, him to keep bringing me business but I also want him to tell other people he works with to bring me the business. And you

Marketpros.com

can do this and you can grow business by being the expert, especially if you pick a niche.

You know, asked the question the first day. How do I find clients? How do I do this if I don't have a lot of money to invest? You put the time in, you learn your market and pick a niche, okay?

Kerry Jackson: Again, we have what? The three things that we talked about the two days which were your time. That's all a Real Estate Professional has, isn't it, Robert?

Robert Drake: Absolutely.

Kerry Jackson: They all they have is their time, their knowledge and heart. That's all they have. They don't have all these properties. They don't own themselves, they just have those three things. Absolutely right. Now, you were talking about going back to when you were dealing with all these agents. And having trust with all these agents not knowing, that kind of blind faith, I guess, you were saying. That you weren't sure how you were going to look after them but you did. And that sort of, you know, you became very successful. You ended up making it work with the other agents in that area where you handled the properties for the guy, the investor that you're working with. And in doing that, now you can...

If you don't mind go on the part where you met me. And again, it was blind faith, the same sort of thing. And where we've developed a relationship now. A close relationship in real estate where we have... Where we can trust each other now and it's very profitable for both of us, so... You want to go ahead and say it?

Robert Drake: We'll be back up a little, I'll back up to July of 2013. So where the story starts.

Kerry Jackson: Okay.

Robert Drake: There was a broker from Miami.

Kerry Jackson: Right.

Robert Drake: ... that came over and was trying to package up lots. And I'm not even sure how he got my name or how he heard of me.

Kerry Jackson: Right.

Robert Drake: So we got together and he had, in my mind, a lot of crazy ideas. You know, I needed his, I need a block about five hundred lots because he want to tack on a hundred and hundred fifty thousand on the back. And you know, be able not let the guys know that he's buying it...

Kerry Jackson: Like Walt Disney?

Robert Drake: Yes, pretty much. I said, "It doesn't work like that." I mean, the chances of me finding one person that wants five hundred lots, that I can buy at the right price to I mean, can it happen? Sure. But is it going to happen today? No. Might happen for five years. I don't know. It doesn't happen like that." So I stepped back, "I could probably put together a package. We take some money and accumulating and get you." "No, no, no, can't do it that way." Because he wanted to make the home run. So the deal didn't go very well and I was entirely getting tired of dealing with this guy, to be honest with you because he kept calling with all these crazy ideas. But I did, I kept working with him. And one day, he calls me up and says, "Robert, I got something. You have a package?" I said, "Yes, I just got this package for three point seven." "Because I've got a guy, he's got five million dollars. I'm bringing his bank statement with me." "Okay. Now, you got my attention."

Marketpros.com

	So he brings down a fellow by the name, will get more to the story. Because Kerry. Because I'd love to tell you when she met him, I'd love to go there after. What her initial thoughts of him were. What do you think of an investor? Big, High-power. This guy probably got a hundred fifty million bucks to invest and he has properties all over the place. But let me keep the story... Go on...
Kerry Jackson:	The names are being changed because we don't want to reveal his true identity so, okay. So, go ahead.
Robert Drake:	Okay, anyway, he brings me this client, him and I hit off right away. I drove him all over Cape Coral. I gave him, I told him in four hours of driving around, everything, in an abbreviated version. And we started talking about, what to buy, what my opinions on buying, what he thinks. Over the next month and half, he ended up buying, I think thirty-five, forty properties from me.
Kerry Jackson:	Wow.
Robert Drake:	So, over the next couple of months. We did some stuff and I would do his stuff, I've got other investors I'm working with. Then he would call to have any good stuff and I would really want to have a good deal. It always went to him because he had the money to pull the trigger real quick. You work with investors, you find the guys that have cash, it's about money and speed. Because if it's a great deal... Look, I'm not going to be all windows about it forever. You've got a short window at time, okay? Anyway, he had brought some properties up in Santa Rosa Beach, Miramar Beach, Panama City Beach with some partners... as I won't get in too

much details with that. But I'm up there, he calls me, "Robert, I've got problems. I've got some partners that I got involved with. I don't understand what's going on, I need help. Will you go there with me? Now, that's eight and half hour drive for me. He flies down to Miami, drives over to me. We've only spent some pieces together. We talked on the phone, he's English is a little broken, so we have trouble. It's much better when we're together. But we built this bond of trust. That he wanted me to run an area that I have no idea with. I've been once, to visit my parents in Pensacola Beach, about eight years ago. So this is how much I know about the **area**.

So, we drove up then we met with all the players. And it was an interesting stories so we can sit. I'll tell you stories next month about that. But...

Kerry Jackson: Did you meet with a bunch of other Real Estate Professionals when you were there? Or did you approach any?

Robert Drake: My intent was. The first trip my intent was but I got so overwhelmed with the engineers and the attorneys and all the stuff that was going on. Really, he just couldn't handle all his properties. We're talking about eight million dollars worth of properties up there. And I have got to get my hands wrapped around all these properties and I have no idea. I don't even know what street I'm on most of the time.

He start talking to me, "You know, right on the corner by the ?." "Yes, okay." I couldn't even find the Walmart**.**

Kerry Jackson: Wow.

Robert Drake: I'm overwhelmed, okay? And I'm driving back. And my client gets on the road and he was off to Mississippi because he goes like nobody's

Marketpros.com

business. And all of a sudden, I get a call from calls me, "This is Robert, I'm driving." "You need to call this woman now." I'm like, "What? Okay..." So I'm driving, I'm writing down this phone number. "And when she calls, she wants to buy one of these properties, the one in Panama City Beach, as a matter of fact." So I talked to Kerry on the phone. At this point, I'm no idea, How the heck did you find this guy's cellphone number? So anyway, I will let Kerry fill in her piece in and then we kind of fill out the rest of the blanks on the story. So how did you get to me? Because you did some work there.

Kerry Jackson: What I was doing was I actually, it started on my end. It started with a customer of mine that I sold a home too. And we talked about him investing in the area after he bought his home. He lived in Mississippi, he owned a company there. I knew he had the whereabouts to be an investor in the area and he had talked about wanting to do it. And talking to me he said, "We'll what I'd really like to do is build a whole subdivision." "That's a real home run for a Real Estate Professional." You know you're... it's not just one house, invest in a house. You got a whole subdivision. He says, "Here is the deal though. I want you to find me something that's not listed." Number one which is kind of hard because it takes a lot more work to uncover them. Secondly, he didn't want to pay for the land which he would, in a more difficult to find an owner of some property who was willing to give you the land and be paid for it after you built the houses. I think a lot of agents... I mean, how many agents out there would have said, "You know, have a nice day." And...ignored him

The rest of this story you will find on Youtube.

125

Your USPs Unique Selling Proposition

Why You Need A Compelling USP Your USP sets the strategic direction for your real estate business. It helps you define where your business is going and what you stand for. Your USP is not simply a marketing or advertising thing.

A compelling USP is more than a headline at the top of your ads. Your USP is the backbone of your real estate business and helps you turn people you're talking to into clients. The Absolutely Worst U.S.P's

- Been in business X amount of years. • Lowest prices guaranteed • We can help everyone with everything! • Satisfaction Guaranteed • All customers hear is blah, blah, blah... U.S.P's That Sell Fed-Ex: When it absolutely, positively has to be there next day

- When you had a high priority document that you needed to get somewhere overnight, you choose Fedex.

Raymour & Flanigan: Guaranteed delivery of your furniture in 3 days or less.

- The first furniture retailer in New England to offer 3 day delivery, so if you needed it fast, you chose Raymour.

Domino's: Delivery in 30 minutes or its free.

- If you were hungry and needed pizza fast, then you chose Domino's. The It Factor That Made ALL Those USP's Work!

- Precise enough to echo the prospects thoughts. • Addresses the biggest objection or fear to buying. • Promises to solve one major problem that prospect will pay to have solved.

Marketpros.com

Notes

- Includes the dominant emotion driving the prospect.

- Unique enough to be easily memorable. What Do All Those USP's Have In Common?

- High competition industries and business just like real estate.

- USP's that speak to their target market.

- Most target a niche within a niche.

All were regular, boring products or services

- Furniture • Mail delivery • Pizza

If They Did It, So Can You!

The Simple 3-Step USP Creation Formula

1. Determine what your clients want.

2. Find out which of these needs you can fill.

3. Find a way to clearly state to your prospects that you are the source to fill those needs.

The Absolutely, Necessary Things You Must Have To Make Your USP Compelling!

Compelling U.S.P Ingredient #1

Be unique: A unique service or bundle of services your competitor doesn't have.

Compelling U.S.P Ingredient #2

Be specific: Be precise and specific with your USP statement because it adds credibility and makes it more believable.

Compelling U.S.P Ingredient #3

Marketpros.com

Be relevant: It must be something that is important and compelling to your prospect. If it doesn't connect with your prospect, it won't work.

Compelling U.S.P Ingredient #4

Be believable: Don't offer something so unbelievable that it destined to fail because it's so far out.

Compelling U.S.P Ingredient #5 Be focused: You must be super targeted in what type of prospect you're trying to reach, while at the same time focusing on a target market that will allow you to make a sustainable income.

Compelling U.S.P Ingredient #6 Be concise: Don't waste your prospects time or space in your advertising using more words or images than absolutely necessary. Questions You Must Ask Yourself To Develop A Compelling USP

- What sets my company or business apart from my competitors? • Do my homes sell faster? For more money? • Do my buyers save money or time? • Am I more expensive or less expensive? • Do I have a better system to attract customers? • Am I more aggressive in my marketing programs and strategies? • Do I provide more service? Give better value? Give a better guarantee? Make it easier to do business with me? • What makes me different?

Seven Proven U.S.P. Strategies You Can Use In Your Business Without Lowering Your Prices! U.S.P Strategy #1 Unique Service: This is a USP that highlights a unique and innovative program that you can offer to help people buy or sell a home faster and easier.

- View 6 Homes in One Afternoon With My Sunday Tour of Homes • How to Get the Information on

Homes You Want Without Having to Talk With an Agent • How To Get Advance Notice of Hot New Listings That Match Your Criteria

U.S.P Strategy #7   Unique Marketing Strategy Or Tactic – Is there a unique way of advertising?

Red Bull designed a fleet of cars with a big red can on top and gave out free samples to college students all across the world.

Zip cars are traveling billboards while being used by their customers.

Using this strategy can separate you from your competitors in the mind of your marketplace.

But, Here's The Catch…   No matter how good you're USP is, you must be able to consistently deliver on your promise or you're better off not having a U.S.P!   You MUST Give Customers A Compelling Reason To Buy From Your business! No matter how great you think your product/company/service is, if you don't have a compelling U.S.P., then you are just another faceless agents in a long list of faceless agents. You Know Your U.S.P. Is Good When…

- Clients come in and say the only reason they came in is because of your U.S.P. (not because super low prices.)

- Clients drive by your competitors business's, parks in your competitors parking lot because yours is crowded, just so they could buy from you because your the expert in xxx.

- Customer drives through blizzard/hurricane/flood/fire and risks bodily harm to get to your office because you're the expert in xxx (your U.S.P.)

Marketpros.com

By The Way...

Great U.S.P's allow you to charge premium fees and earn massive profits while your clients love you and feel good about working with you!

With Rare Exception, There's A Market At All Price Points!

Quick Note:

You can have more than one USP. In fact, it's smart to develop a USP for each target market you're going after. Be sure to make it crystal clear what your USP is actually offering. Each USP needs its own marketing campaign and strategy. It's even better if you can create a separate brand for each target market, but that's not always possible.

Use this area to write your ideas for your USP's

_____
_____
_____
_____
_____
_____
_____
_____
_____
_____
_____
_____
_____
_____
_____
_____
_____
_____
_____
_____

_____
_____
_____
_____
_____
_____

The Harsh Reality…

If an effective U.S.P. is so powerful, then why do most real estate agents not do it?

- **It's Different** – Coming up with a good USP requires you to take a step back and think about your real estate business dramatically different than what they're doing now.

- **Laziness/Too Comfortable** – Refusing to develop new products, new marketing strategies, new sales techniques etc. or anything else that takes real work.

- **Too Stubborn** – Refusing to listen to customers, staff, marketplace, legislation etc.

- **Ignorance** – Didn't take the time to go out and seek answers to their business problems. Once You Develop A U.S.P Put Your U.S.P. Everywhere! Business Cards

- **Voicemail** • Business Signs (Inside and outside) • Phone Greeting • Letterhead and Stationary. • Sales Receipts • Website • Brochures • Anywhere else you can think of!!!

Marketpros.com

For More tips to become a MarketPro™, visit MarketPros.com:

Giving real estate professionals a place to be acknowledged as one of the most trusted in their community and in the real estate industry because they have earned it through their experience and by displaying the same core values of a certified Marketpro.

Thank you for reading my 1st Book and hopefully there was something in this book that will encourage you to become a Marketpro so the world can know absolutely you are a professional in the Real Estate Industry they can Trust.

About the Author:

Kerry started her first business at the early age of 8 when she started a paper route in Toronto, Canada. Building several routes and selling them for a profit, Kerry learned the value of hard work, determination and the entrepreneurial spirit took hold. A Right Brained Canadian born and raised in Toronto Canada moved to Florida in 1990 after a hostile takeover of a Grocery chain she was co founder and the HOLLY of Holly Home Supermarkets.

After heading to Florida for a month to decide what she wanted to do next she quickly gravitated to The Bay County Florida area where she worked Business to Business Sales in a couple of different industries including the Telecommunications field as the Internet blossomed. After 5 years of that she started in the Real Estate Industry (in 1999) as an Investor and quickly changed careers to becoming a Licensed Florida Realtor. Started her own Brokerage in around 2001 and became one of the top 3 Realtors in Bay County for 2004 selling more than 68 million and close to it in 2005 ,2006, 2007 the following few years.

She has gone from Rags to Riches and back again as she lost everything in the 2009 Real estate downfall and has been building her way back from Bankruptcy, divorce and a near death illness both spiritually, emotionally and financially by selling Real estate from the Inside out. I build relationships and help match Sellers with Buyers and Buyers with what they want and need. What I learn from everyday experiences in this industry I like to share by speaking. I enjoy coaching agents to work from the Inside out with their Marketing techniques and to just help people with what they need help with. Knowing that when you do this, the money will come, even if it comes through a different channel.

I teach businesses and Realtors how to Create, Build and Maintain Relationships that will stay with them throughout their lifetime. Dedicated to a successful outcome for all my clients and fellow agents I cross paths with and doing what it takes with proper Habits, Ethics, Attitude and Resilience to gain Trust.

Marketpros.com

Made in the USA
Columbia, SC
30 September 2023